FORTRESS • 84

CHINESE WALLED CITIES 221 BC–AD 1644

STEPHEN TURNBULL

ILLUSTRATED BY STEVE NOON

Series editors Marcus Cowper and Nikolai Bogdanovic

First published in 2009 by Osprey Publishing
Midland House, West Way, Botley, Oxford OX2 0PH, UK
443 Park Avenue South, New York, NY 10016, USA
E-mail: info@ospreypublishing.com

ISBN: 978-184603-381-0

Editorial by Ilios Publishing Ltd, Oxford UK (www.iliospublishing.com)
Cartography by the Map Studio, Romsey, UK
Page layout by Ken Vail Graphic Design, Cambridge, UK (kvgd.com)
Typeset in Sabon and Myriad Pro
Index by Glyn Sutcliffe
Originated by PPS Grasmere, Leeds, UK
Printed and bound in China through Bookbuilders

09 10 11 12 13   10 9 8 7 6 5 4 3 2 1

A CIP catalogue record for this book is available from the British Library.

FOR A CATALOGUE OF ALL BOOKS PUBLISHED BY OSPREY MILITARY AND AVIATION PLEASE CONTACT:

Osprey Direct, c/o Random House Distribution Center, 400 Hahn Road, Westminster, MD 21157
Email: uscustomerservice@ospreypublishing.com

Osprey Direct, The Book Service Ltd, Distribution Centre, Colchester Road, Frating Green, Colchester, Essex, CO7 7DW
E-mail: customerservice@ospreypublishing.com

www.ospreypublishing.com

DEDICATION

To Darren Ashmore, with thanks for his friendship and support, Akita International University 2008.

ARTIST'S NOTE

Readers may care to note that the original paintings from which the colour plates in this book were prepared are available for private sale. All reproduction copyright whatsoever is retained by the Publishers. All enquiries should be addressed to:

Steve Noon, 50 Colchester Avenue, Penylan, Cardiff CF23 9BP, United Kingdom

The Publishers regret that they can enter into no correspondence upon this matter.

THE FORTRESS STUDY GROUP (FSG)

The object of the FSG is to advance the education of the public in the study of all aspects of fortifications and their armaments, especially works constructed to mount or resist artillery. The FSG holds an annual conference in September over a long weekend with visits and evening lectures, an annual tour abroad lasting about eight days, and an annual Members' Day.

The FSG journal FORT is published annually, and its newsletter Casemate is published three times a year. Membership is international. For further details, please contact:

The Secretary, c/o 6 Lanark Place, London W9 1BS, UK

Website: www.fsgfort.com

THE WOODLAND TRUST

Osprey Publishing are supporting the Woodland Trust, the UK's leading woodland conservation charity, by funding the dedication of trees.

CONTENTS

CHINESE FORTIFIED CITIES 1500 BC–AD 1644

INTRODUCTION

China possesses the world's longest tradition of fortified buildings and settlements, yet the study of this has always been hampered by an understandable tendency for any researcher's eyes to be irresistibly drawn towards the magnificent and romantic structure that is the Great Wall of China. This can unfortunately take one's attention away from the fine city walls that have protected not only China's capitals, but almost every urban community, for many centuries. Although nowadays they are often pierced by modern roads and railways, and sometimes have even been demolished to make room for them (Beijing being a notorious example), extensive sections of the walls of several of China's fortified cities still stand as splendid memorials of ancient defensive systems. There has, however, been a welcome trend within recent years for wholesale and usually sensitive restoration, so that many now look as formidable as they ever did and are often more rewarding to study than the famous Great Wall, because even though the defences of the finest fortified cities may appear to the casual eye as no more than the Great Wall in miniature, this is usually only in terms of the wall's overall length. Other details are sometimes finer, because in contrast to the sometimes monotonous repetition

The Shang dynasty wall made from rammed earth at Zhengzhou. These are probably the most ancient surviving walls in China, and are used today almost as a public park.

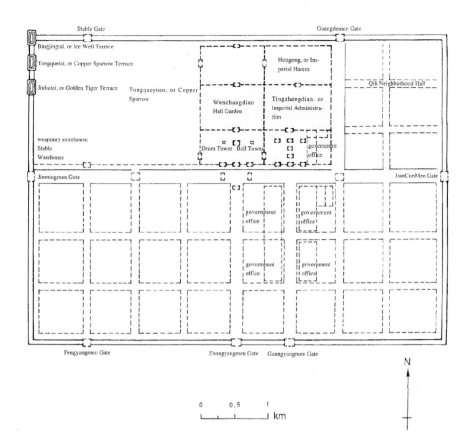

Stable Gate

Guangdemen Gate

Bingjingtai, or Ice Well Terrace

Tongquetai, or Copper Sparrow Terrace

Jinhutai, or Golden Tiger Terrace

Tongqueyuan, or Copper Sparrow

Hougong, or Imperial Harem

Qili Neighborhood Hall

Wenchangdian Hall Garden

Tingzhengdian, or Imperial Administration

weaponry storehouse

Stable

Warehouse

Drum Tower   Bell Tower

government office

Jinmingmen Gate

JianCunMen Gate

government office

government office

government office

government office

Fengyangmen Gate

Zhongyangmen Gate   Guangyangmen Gate

N

0   0.5   1

km

A plan of Ye Cheng, the capital established by Cao Cao, one of the protagonists in the Three Kingdoms Period in AD 213. It was located south of the Zhangshui River in Hebei. The city was built on strict military lines, and a transverse road divided the *cheng* into two parts. The northern section was where the ruling class had their residences, and included a further wall round the palace *cheng* and the three Bronze Sparrow Pavilions on top of the north-western wall, which served as places of entertainment in peacetime and as defences in wartime. (After Ishihara Heizo)

of defensive features on the Great Wall, the city walls have a variety and an intricacy about them that their big brother lacks. Nowhere do they defer to it in width or height, nor in the splendour of their gateways and their towers. Also, unlike much of the Great Wall, Chinese city walls saw a lively operational history, an uncomfortable fact of life for the inhabitants who depended upon them so often in the nation's violent history.

As this work concentrates on the fortified cities themselves rather than on the means used to defend or attack them, the reader is referred to my two volumes in the Osprey New Vanguard series, *Siege Weapons of the Far East (1) AD 612–1300* and *Siege Weapons of the Far East (2) AD 960–1644* for details of such devices. These should be read particularly in connection with the section that follows on operational history.

The Chinese dynasties and their fortified cities

The ubiquitous presence of walls around Chinese cities, towns and even villages is apparent to the most casual visitor to China. As the author of an article on Chinese architecture for *Encyclopaedia Britannica* observed many years ago:

Walls, walls, and yet again walls, form the framework of every Chinese city. They surround it, they divide it into lots and compounds, they mark more than any other structures the basic features of the Chinese communities. There is no real city in China without a surrounding wall, a condition which is indeed expressed by the fact that the Chinese used the same word *cheng* for a city and a city wall; there is no such thing as a city without a wall. It would be just as inconceivable as a house without a roof.

Part of the eastern wall of Datong. A considerable proportion of the circuit of rammed earth walls of this ancient former capital has survived, and may be followed around the city. In most places courtyard dwellings are built directly on to the wall's surface.

He goes on to note the presence of a wall around even very small villages, then returns to the situation of the defended city:

> Many a city in north-western China which has been partly demolished by war and famine and fire, where no house is left standing and where no human being lives, still retains its crenellated walls with their gates and watchtowers. Those bare brick walls, sometimes rising over a moat, or again simply from the open level ground where the view of the distance is unblocked by buildings, often tell more of the ancient greatness of the city than the houses and temples.

To this observation of 'bare brick walls' may be added the opportunity to see, and even walk along, some considerable remains of rammed earth walls that are an amazing three millennia old. They lie where the Yellow River was to become the cradle of Chinese civilization and are to be found in the Shang dynasty (*c.* 1520–1030 BC) city of Zhengzhou. From the time of the Shang onwards successive dynasties were to be marked by the creation of new capitals, often on sites used by former dynasties, and their fortification by strong city walls. Indeed, the story of the rise and fall of successive dynasties can be told through the history of the capitals they selected. Thus the Shang were overthrown by the Zhou, who expanded their kingdom west of the Yellow River into Shaanxi province, where they made a capital in the vicinity of modern Xi'an. They ruled through a hierarchy of powerful vassals, whose activities slowly reduced the Zhou power and forced their rulers to move to a new capital at Luoyang in 771 BC, from where later Zhou rulers exercised only a symbolic authority.

Four hundred years of conflict between petty states and kingdoms ensued, to which are given the names of the Spring and Autumn and the Warring States periods. The fighting came to an end with the triumph of China's first emperor Qin Shihuang Di in 221 BC, who ruled from Xianyang, just north of Xi'an, and is best known today for the 'terracotta army' that guards his tomb. The Qin Emperor's reign did not last long, and in 206 BC the rebel warlord Liu Bang founded the Han dynasty. He built a completely new capital on the site of Xi'an, to which was given the name Chang'an. It took two major efforts to build the wall – the first in 194 BC, the second five years later – involving the

The capture of Chang'an in
AD 617 by Li Yuan, who was to
become Emperor Gaozu of the
Tang dynasty, from a painting
in the museum in the Tang
Paradise theme park in Xi'an.

mobilization of tens of thousands of labourers. The resulting wall was an irregular rectangle that was almost square, its perimeter being 25.5km. There were three triple gateways on each side with their own towers. The Han dynasty greatly expanded their domains, until infighting led to problems and the setting up of the Eastern Han dynasty at Luoyang. Chang'an was abandoned, and was described by a later traveller as 'overgrown with rank grass, and haunted by foxes, hares and pheasants'. Luoyang, however, was quite magnificent, with a rectangular layout measuring 4.3km by 3.7km.

Nearly four centuries of sporadic conflict separate the collapse of the Han dynasty and the reunification of China under the Sui dynasty in AD 589. By the end of the Eastern Han Period local gentry, clansmen and villagers would join together and built forts for protection. These *wu bi* are the nearest we

The two-storey pavilion on top
of the western gate at Kaifeng.
This is a typical construction
found in many sites. Details
of the brick *nuqian* (parapets)
round the top of the wall may
also be noted.

come in Chinese history to the European concept of a castle. They were built in remote country areas, were square in shape and had a high surrounding wall with gates to the front and back and watchtowers at each of the four corners. No ruins of any such fort have survived, and this cursory description has been gained only from unearthed pottery and murals.

From AD 200 onwards the 'Three Kingdoms' of Wei, Wu and Shu fought for supremacy in a long and complicated rivalry that provided a rich vein of legend and romance in which fortifications played a part. For example, Cao Cao built Ye Cheng in Hebei, which included in its design three 'Bronze Sparrow Pavilions' that served for amusement during peacetime and as fortifications in times of war. Several minor southern dynasties fortified and used the site of modern Nanjing, which was defended by the mighty Yangzi River. Far to the north the Tuoba Wei established the Wei dynasty based at Datong in Shanxi, where they left behind a wonderful series of rock carvings along with a beaten earth wall, but in AD 534 their empire collapsed, and several classic sieges took place around the fortified cities of their bewildering array of competing successors. In AD 581 General Yang Jian unified the fragmented northern states, and then went on to conquer southern China and found the Sui dynasty, taking the name Emperor Wen Di. The Sui dynasty rebuilt Luoyang, but chose the site of Xi'an for their capital. Known as Da Xingcheng it was protected by a vast outer wall 35km in extent. Wen Di's successor Yang Di achieved an engineering feat of a different kind when he ordered the construction of the Grand Canal to transport produce from south of the Yangzi River.

In AD 618 Yang Di was assassinated following a military revolt led by General Li Yuan, who became Emperor Gaozu of the Tang dynasty. Xi'an, then known as Chang'an, became the glorious capital of this celebrated

The considerable width and height of the Ming walls of Xi'an are revealed in this view from a corner tower.

The principal fortified cities of China

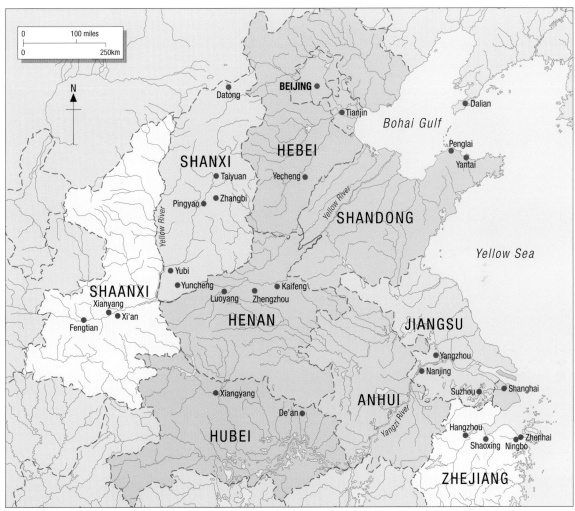

dynasty, with outer walls measuring 9.72km east to west by 8.65km north to south, covering a total area of 83km². Like the Sui, the Tang retained Luoyang as their eastern capital. So influential was the Tang dynasty and the culture it supported that Chang'an was to become the model for capital cities in Japan and Korea.

The Tang's longevity was to be in marked contrast to the so-called Five Dynasties and Ten Kingdoms that came and went between AD 907 and AD 960 until a coup finally put General Song Tai Zu on the throne as the first emperor of the Song dynasty. The Song capital was Kaifeng on the Yellow River basin, the last of the imperial capitals to be built in this region. The Song control was not however complete, because they had to compete with the Kitan Liao dynasty, which ruled over parts of northern China. Also, in northern Manchuria, beyond the territory held by the Liao, tribes known as the Jurchens had risen to power. They rebelled against the Liao in AD 1114 and the next year adopted the dynastic name of Jin. The Song, hoping to regain territories lost to the Liao, unwisely allied themselves to the Jin to help in the destruction of the Liao, which was achieved in AD 1125. However, when the Song showed dissatisfaction with their share of the spoils the Jin

A fortified city of the Later Han dynasty under attack by the Yellow Turbans in AD 184

continued their aggressive moves to the south, and early in AD 1127 captured Kaifeng. From this time on Song hegemony was limited to southern China, so that the dynasty then became known as Southern Song. For a while the Southern Song continued to fight back against the Jin, and conducted operations from the safety of their new capital of Hangzhou from AD 1135 onwards. The old eastern wall of Hangzhou was strengthened by brick cladding on the inside and outside and was given 13 gates with watchtowers on top and a semi-circular enceinte in front. Moats were dug and planted with trees.

In AD 1153 the Jin moved their capital to Zhongdu, the site of present-day Beijing, but at the beginning of the 13th century both dynasties began to suffer the depredations caused by the Mongols, who preferred to deal with the main field forces of their enemies before advancing far into hostile territory where there were likely to be fortified places. As Genghis Khan's unsuccessful siege of the Xixia capital in AD 1209 was to illustrate, the Mongols' whirlwind mounted operations tended to come to a halt at a well-defended town wall, but, showing the military ability for which they were to become renowned, these fierce horsemen rapidly acquired the techniques of siegecraft. This included making extensive use of captives skilled in siege technology.

The Mongol advance against the Jin continued in AD 1212 with a move against Datong, where Genghis Khan was wounded by an arrow, but much more effort was directed towards capturing Zhongdu, so in AD 1214 the Jin emperor decided to move the imperial residence to the old Song capital of Kaifeng, which was protected from the north by the Yellow River. The Mongols saw this as a provocation, so the siege of Zhongdu was pressed forward with even greater vigour. The walls of Zhongdu then measured 24km around and reached a height of 12m. Twelve gates gave access to the city, and there were 900 towers and three lines of moats. Several Mongol assaults failed, so the decision was made to let starvation do the work for them. By the summer of AD 1215 there were reports of cannibalism, and in June the Jin commander abandoned his post and fled to join the emperor in Kaifeng.

In AD 1227 Genghis Khan died, which gave the Jin some respite from Mongol attacks until Ogedei Khan resumed operations by sending his famous general Subadai against Kaifeng in AD 1231. The Jin defended themselves using iron-cased bombs and fire lances, but the city fell the following year after a celebrated siege. The Jin empire finally surrendered in AD 1234.

The Mongols pressed forward their conquest of the Southern Song from AD 1254 onwards in a huge operation hindered temporarily by the death of Mongke Khan in AD 1259. The effort was resumed by Khubilai Khan in AD 1265, and the campaign which followed proved to be a colossal military undertaking that faced numerous obstacles. The Mongol armies were not used to the climate or the terrain of the south, and were also faced with formidable

A A FORTIFIED CITY OF THE LATER HAN DYNASTY UNDER ATTACK BY THE YELLOW TURBANS IN AD 184

During the waning years of the Han dynasty serious rebellions arose under three brothers, Zhang Jue, Zhang Liang and Zhang Bao. They were charismatic religious leaders, and promised their followers that the azure heaven of the Han would be replaced by a yellow heaven under the Yellow Emperor, as Zhang Jue styled himself. Their followers wore yellow turbans or headscarves. Here they are seen attacking the rammed earth walls of a Han dynasty fortified city.

The walls are made from layers of rammed loess painstakingly hammered down in layers and then coated with oily yellow clay. The successive layers can be seen on the outer surfaces of the walls, which are protected with battlements above an overhanging lip. So strong are the walls that an elaborate gatehouse with a tower could be raised above it. The rebels are poorly armed and have only scaling ladders with which to attack the city.

walled cities such as Xiangyang on the Han River, which was besieged for five years between AD 1268 and AD 1273. But the extent of the Mongol conquests allowed them to bring back new siege weapons to China, of which the most important was the Muslim counterweight trebuchet. It was first used in China at Xiangyang in AD 1272. Projectiles could now be launched weighing ten times more than any stone thrown hitherto, and one particular shot (perhaps exceeding 90kg) launched on target brought down the drum tower of Xiangyang with a 'noise like thunder'. A commentator noted that 'the projectiles were several feet in diameter, and when they fell to the earth, they made a hole three or four feet deep'. Realizing the tremendous advantage that he now possessed, Khubilai wasted no time in sending these new weapons against Hangzhou. Bayan, one of the most gifted of all Mongol leaders, was chosen to lead the advance. He crossed the Yangzi River in January AD 1275 and met the Song forces in a series of battles where the Mongol superiority in artillery made a decisive difference. Bayan went on to bombard and take Yangzhou, 'breaking down temples, towers and halls'. Bayan's army occupied one town after another, some surrendering as soon as the army came in sight with its fearsome counterweight trebuchets, and finally Hangzhou fell. In AD 1279 the last remnants of the Song dynasty were eliminated, and Khubilai Khan became the first emperor of the new Yuan (Mongol) dynasty.

The Yuan dynasty became the first rulers in the history of the world to make use of the metal-barrelled cannon, which appeared in Chinese sieges decades before similar weapons were being employed in Europe. But even cannon were not sufficient to save the Yuan when a rebel army captured Nanjing in AD 1356 and, with this as their first capital, began a campaign to overthrow the Mongol dynasty. City walls again played an important role, and started falling to cannon, as at the siege of Shaoxing in AD 1359. The rebels took Beijing in AD 1368, and that same year their leader Zhu Yuan Zhang proclaimed himself the first emperor of the Ming dynasty.

The Ming capital was transferred to Beijing early in the 15th century. To some it was an act of madness to locate the dynastic capital so close to the unstable northern frontier, even though Beijing was to be protected by fine walls. The Ming are, of course, better known for the Great Wall of China rather than for the stone and brick walls of similar design with which they surrounded Beijing during four busy years from AD 1407 onwards. Similar rebuilding efforts were undertaken in many other Chinese cities such as Xi'an, Kaifeng and Zhengzhou. It grew into an ambitious programme that drew on earlier models of fortification from the Song, Tang or even Han periods to be found at or near the sites.

Yet even Ming dynasty walls, the high-water mark of Chinese fortified city design, were insufficient to save the Ming from collapse in AD 1644. Their successors from the Manchu Qing dynasty were originally Jurchens, the same tribes whose Jin dynasty had made their own contribution to siege weaponry by introducing iron-cased bombs in AD 1221. In AD 1616 their leader Nurhachi took the title of emperor of the Later Jin dynasty, and two years later openly attacked the Ming and captured part of Liaodong. Following Nurhachi's death in battle in AD 1626 his son Abahai led expeditions against the Ming and broke through the passes in the Great Wall on several occasions between AD 1629 and AD 1638. In AD 1636 he proclaimed the Qing dynasty, and was able to take Beijing in AD 1644 largely because the commander of Shanhaiguan invited him and his army inside the Great Wall to help against the attacks of a Chinese rebel. When Beijing fell the Ming dynasty came to an end, and with it came the end of the greatest period of wall construction. The Qing preserved and repaired the Ming walls but added little to them. Yet they did not destroy them. That was to be the curse of the 20th century in China, a process from which a few examples are now slowly recovering.

CHRONOLOGY

c. 1520 BC–*c.* 1030 BC	Shang dynasty.
771 BC	Zhou build Luoyang.
722 BC to 480 BC	Spring and Autumn periods.
480 BC–221 BC	Warring States Period.
279 BC	Siege of Jimo.
221 BC	Unification under Qin.
206 BC	Liu Bang founds Han dynasty.
194 BC	Han Chang'an begun.
AD 220–26	Three Kingdoms Period.
AD 546	Siege of Yubi.
AD 548	Siege of Jiankang (Nanjing).
AD 581	Sui reunification of the north.
AD 618	Tang dynasty founded.
AD 634	New palace complex added to Chang'an.
AD 757	Siege of Suiyang.
AD 783	Siege of Fengtian by rebels against the Tang.
AD 906	Fall of Tang.
AD 960	Northern Song.
AD 1125	Song/Jin alliance defeats Liao.
AD 1127	Fall of Kaifeng, establishment of Southern Song.
AD 1132	Siege of De'an.
AD 1153	Jin set up capital at Zhongdu (Beijing).
AD 1207	Sieges of Xiangyang and De'an.
AD 1215	Zhongdu falls to Mongols.
AD 1232	Capture of Kaifeng by the Mongols.
AD 1268–73	Siege of Xiangyang.
AD 1341	Fire destroys much of Hangzhou.
AD 1351	Panmen (Watergate) of Suzhou rebuilt.
AD 1356	Ming rebels capture Nanjing.
AD 1366	Ming walls of Nanjing begun.
AD 1359	Siege of Shaoxing.
AD 1407	Ming walls of Beijing started.

| AD **1582** | Bell tower of Xi'an built. |
| AD **1644** | Qing take Beijing. |

DESIGN AND DEVELOPMENT

Location and layout

In the brief descriptions above of the city walls of successive dynasties a certain similarity in overall design may be noted. This is no coincidence, because the overall ideas of city planning, including size of walls, the number of gates and the layout of roads, was determined by set rules, which were adhered to right through to the Ming and Qing dynasties. A Chinese walled city, therefore, tended to present a uniform appearance. The principle of 'five gates and three royal courts' on a central axis leading to the imperial palace complex was the accepted layout for the capital according to the accepted wisdom of what could be defended, and from the Sui dynasty onwards this layout evolved into a threefold system of palatial *cheng*, inner *cheng* and outer *cheng* in order to guard from rebellion within as well as external threats.

A favourable geographical position was of utmost importance in selecting any site. In the early Han period, Liu Bang was advised to found his capital at Chang'an because it was backed by a mountain and guarded in front by a river, and thus difficult to approach. Xi'an's enviable location led to it being chosen as capital by ten different dynasties over a period of 1,000 years, while six dynasties chose Luoyang because it was 'prime terrain under heaven'. Kaifeng had communication routes running from it like the spokes of a wheel, while Nanjing's location was likened to a coiled dragon or a crouching tiger.

The location of a city with a river in front and a mountain behind is a principle that may be derived from feng shui with its notions of lucky directions, but we must not jump to the conclusion that only feng shui was involved in the siting of Chinese walled cities. Such considerations were certainly applied to later attempts to manipulate space and structure for specific purposes, but there were other considerations besides feng shui in selecting an original site. Some were no less mystical, however, because from the time of the Zhou dynasty onwards the ideal city shape was the square, which may well derive from the belief that the heavens were round and the earth, with its four cardinal points, was square. This shape of city would become the preferred norm for the flat plains of northern China, but in areas of rough territory the square form was usually replaced by one of irregular shape, determined in most cases simply by topographical conditions, as in the classic example of Nanjing. The size of the walled area and the degree of elaboration of wall construction were normally directly proportional to the rank of the city in the administrative hierarchy from the capital city downwards. An outer wall (*guo*) was often erected later to enclose settlements that had spread outside the *cheng*.

B THE CONSTRUCTION OF A RAMMED EARTH CITY WALL AROUND THE TIME OF THE TANG DYNASTY IN AD 700

In this plate we see compressed into one scene the different sequences involved in building a rammed earth wall at the time of the Tang dynasty (AD 618–906). On top of a foundation of rammed stones the successive layers of loess are rammed down within removable wooden shutters in the mode of construction known as *hangtu*. This is exactly the same method as was used during the Han dynasty in the artwork on page 10, but now the walls are being encased with fired bricks. The bricks are brought to the site by hand, while earth is carried in wheelbarrows or on yokes. Overseers look on as the hundreds of workmen go about their tasks. Even their womenfolk are pressed into service.

The construction of a rammed earth city wall around the time of the Tang dynasty in AD 700

Building city walls

The most ancient form of walling in China was *hangtu* (rammed or tamped earth), whereby successive layers of loess were compacted within removable wooden shuttering, much like that used to confine modern concrete while it sets. Loess is a windblown deposit found in great abundance in China and derived from glacial clays and outwash. It has accumulated over a vast area of China over the past 10,000 years since the Ice Age. Loess can also have bits of shell in it from snails, and these can dissolve to form cement as calcium carbonate; thus, walls made from rammed loess were self-cementing and the clay within it would respond well to ramming. The loess was taken from at least 10cm below the surface to minimize the likelihood of including seeds or grasses within the mixture. The ramming tools had either a heavy wooden head or one made of stone and wooden shafts. The layers produced by ramming were about 20cm thick, and could be built up to 6m high. It was customary to dig a trench and use rubble stone without binding material as the foundations, and to spread a layer of thin bamboo between each section to facilitate the drying process. Such layers are clearly visible in extant examples where an applied outer surface of clay has weathered away.

Hangtu was a method that produced walls that were simple but strong, but large city walls built using rammed earth were also very heavy, so far more extensive foundations had to be prepared. Compacted rubble was used for the foundations of small- or medium-sized city walls otherwise blocks of dressed stone, such as those that appear along the Great Wall, or simply bedrock provided a secure base.

This large, surviving section of the western wall of Datong shows the use of brick cladding on the inner surface of the earth core.

The inner wall at Kaifeng was not clad in brick, and reveals the successive layers of rammed earth along its sloping side.

Wherever possible the raw materials were sourced locally to save on manpower costs for transportation, which was often literally provided by man power – either one man carrying a shoulder pole with a basket at each end, or two men sharing a heavier load. Goats and donkeys were also pressed into service. The excavation of a moat or ditch (*chi*) round a city was often a welcome by-product brought about by the nearby supply of raw materials. Moats were often dry, but in southern China water courses were frequently brought into play to provide a wet moat.

As early as the Zhou dynasty rammed earth walls were being enclosed by bricks on their outer surface. These bricks were not fired until the early Han dynasty, and it is only with the Tang dynasty that we find fired bricks being used for this purpose in city walls. At Kaifeng examples still exist along the city wall where brick is used for the outer surface of the wall, while the inner face is buttressed with a wide angle of rammed earth. Stone and brick parapets, called *nuqian* (literally, female walls) were frequently added round the outer rim of a wall as plain walls or battlements. High standards were expected in wall construction, and harsh penalties were meted out if they were not attained. According to Jin Zai Ji:

Halian Bobo authorized Chi Yu He Li, master builder, to build a *cheng* using clay. Its quality was tested by having an owl peck at it. An incision an inch deep sufficed for the builder to be executed; one less deep, for the person in charge of the owl to be killed. Among other testing methods was that of shooting an arrow at a newly built wall. If it failed to pierce the wall the latter was considered to be of good quality. Should the opposite be true, the wall had to be demolished and rebuilt.

With the Ming dynasty we begin to see the extensive use of fired brick walls around a rammed rubble core that was to be the keynote of the Great Wall. The bricks, which were about four times as large as a modern house brick, were produced by the thousand from numerous kilns, some of which still exist near Great Wall sites. In the firing process clay loses water and the silica starts to fuse with new chemical products. Dehydration is the most important factor in producing a good brick. They were bound together using lime mortar, within which was the 'secret ingredient' of glutinous rice paste found in the mortar of the Great Wall. This increased both the strength and the fusion properties of the mortar, and in some places on the Great Wall the bricks have eroded faster than the mortar between them.

Ming city walls were wider at their base than at the top to give stability. Strong foundations were very important, and in some places, such as Nanjing, there was a layer of bedrock beneath the surface which could provide a base. Otherwise an artificial base was usually made from large, dressed granite blocks brought to the location, although some dressing may have been done on site. They may have been dovetailed for stability, and the inner blocks were tapered inwards to provide an irregular shape around which the infill could settle. The infill was a firmly rammed core of the local loess mixed with coarse sand, gravel and rubble.

The neatest brickwork of all was to be found on the upper surfaces of city walls where the final 'skin' has a gentle camber and the joints are as watertight as possible. The highest grade of Ming wall had pavements of carefully mortared brick or stone where rainwater drained away quickly to avoid erosion. Stone drainage spouts were placed only on the inside of the walls so that vegetation growth, which would provide cover to raiders, was inhibited on the enemy side. The walkways along the tops of the wall were often very wide. Xi'an's city walls have the appearance of a paved road.

Gates and towers

No element of a city wall's defences was more important or more visually prominent than its gates. In most cities one could expect to find at least four gates located at the four cardinal points, each bearing some mystic significance in addition to its defensive properties. The simplest gate was usually a dark and forbidding arched tunnel through the wall, either recessed into the wall or protruding from it. More complex designs (*wengcheng*, so-called from their resemblance to an urn) were provided for the main entrances to the city, and these had more elaborate defensive features built into them. Beginning at the ground level, anyone entering would find himself in an enclosed and easily defensible courtyard of sheer walls, from which he was obliged to make a 90-degree turn to enter the city. Bigger gates might have another inner structure, so that a further turn was required. In the case of the huge gate complexes of Nanjing a succession of courtyards slowed down an attacker's entrance. Even though the Nanjing examples were not offset, each successive courtyard could be closed off by means of massive gates, and the visitor was always under surveillance from the parapets of the walls above, all of which were connected for ease of movement by the defenders. Southern China provides example of water gates, of which the Panmen at Suzhou is the finest surviving structure.

Rising above the gates of many cities were to be found gate towers, in which were located the armouries, guardhouse and barracks. These can be formidable buildings of stone and wood, as at Beijing and Xi'an, or lighter and more graceful structures like pavilions or temples, such as can be seen at Pingyao. Smaller towers were built out from the surface of the city wall at regular intervals, as is dramatically illustrated by the long sweep of the walls of Pingyao, which look like an urban Great Wall. Corner towers are often like one of these side towers on a larger scale. Small roofed buildings may be found on top of both types of tower.

The mighty walls of Nanjing, showing the use of different materials within a small area. Sandstone provides the bedrock base, on top of which is a brick wall with stone-faced towers.

The regular layout of many Chinese cities required a grid pattern for the streets and wards within, and this is still to be found in surviving examples. Pingyao provides the classic example of two main streets running between the opposite pairs of gates intersecting in the middle at an elegant tower. A city's drum or bell tower like this would usually be the only tall building within the city, which would otherwise have its silhouette fixed by its outer walls. One notable exception, of course, is the Greater Wild Goose Pagoda in Xi'an, which stands 64m tall.

An interesting 'cutaway' section of a Ming dynasty city wall is presented here thanks to the current reconstruction of the wall around the fortified harbour of Penglai. We see a rammed earth core inside dressed stone and brick, together with drainage spouts and a double parapet.

Moats, river defences and fortified harbours

Chinese fortified cities, of course, were not always defended solely by walls. In southern China in particular, rivers were put into service to provide moats. Nanjing's layout, described in detail later in this work, made good use of its proximity to the Yangzi River. Xiangyang, the site of two celebrated sieges, lay on the Han River and was connected to its sister city Fancheng by a pontoon bridge. The river was put to positive use during the Mongol siege of AD 1268–72 when two heroes of the Southern Song tried to take a relief convoy of 100 paddle-boats laden with clothing and other supplies to the help of the beleaguered city.

A different use of water for defence appears a couple of centuries later in the extensive coastal defences built by the Ming against the notorious *wako* (Japanese pirates). The series of coastal forts, fortified harbours and numerous lookout towers with signalling beacons made the concept into a 'Great Wall of the Sea'. In terms of fortified cities, the programme extended the concept of river defences to that of the fortified harbour. Dengzhou (modern Penglai) Water Fortress, one of its finest examples, was built in 1376. The entrance to the harbour is very narrow and is dominated by a signalling station and a tower not unlike the Old Dragon's Head on the Great Wall, on which cannon were mounted. A rocky breakwater reaching out into the sea further restricted the movement of incoming ships. A vessel entering the harbour then had to pass along a narrow winding channel overlooked by a large multi-storey tower built into the wall that encircles the whole harbour, which was divided into an outer and inner harbour by a further narrow gap crossed by a drawbridge. The whole harbour was surrounded by a high wall with a very impressive land gate. Such cities presented the *wako* with quite a challenge, and it was not until AD 1561, when Xinhua in Fujian province fell to the *wako*, that the whole of a walled city was captured by pirates. Hangzhou, Suzhou and even Nanjing were attacked by pirates on occasions.

This magnificent example of a *wengcheng* gate is at Pingyao. The scale of the edifice is demonstrated by the reproduction cannon on the walkways. The courtyard is crossed at 90 degrees between two dark, arched tunnels. A stone drainage spout protrudes on the left.

The myriad of tiny islands off Ningbo provided lairs for several *wako* gangs, most of whose members were Chinese rather than Japanese. It is therefore surprising to find at Zhenhai, on the coast near Ningbo, one of the best surviving examples of a coastal fort. Of all the fortified places I have studied this comes nearest to the European idea of a castle. It is built on a high wooded promontory overlooking the river estuary and is surrounded by the finest grade of Ming-dynasty brick walls. From Zhenhai, which is entered by an imposing semicircular gateway, it is possible to survey sea traffic for miles around.

THE PRINCIPLES OF DEFENCE

One important consideration to bear in mind when considering city walls as a defensive system is the fact that its walls were the only means of defence that the city possessed. Fortified cities were, of course, common in medieval Europe, but there is one important difference to China: once the attackers had captured the walls of a Chinese city and entered its streets, there was usually no other fortified place within the walls from which further defence could be conducted other than the walls that separated the inner *cheng* from the outer part of the city. In Europe even churches could be fortified alongside private dwellings of the gentry, but in the unified political situation of China no other power existed. Nor, by and large, was there such a thing as a Chinese castle. The town or city was the castle, and was built so that it could serve as protection and refuge, as well as the administrative centre, of the countryside. The nearest equivalent to a European castle would appear to be the fortified manors of wealthy landowners towards the end of the Han dynasty noted earlier, and some garrison villages like Zhang Bi.

City walls were nevertheless formidable barriers; and no less an authority than Son Zi (Sun Tzu) in his classic *Art of War* advised that:

> The worst policy is to attack cities. Attack cities only when there is no alternative, because to prepare big shields and wagons and make ready the necessary arms and equipment require at least three months, and to pile up earthen ramps against the walls requires an additional three months. The general, unable to control his impatience, will order his troops to swarm up the wall like ants, with the result that one third of them will be killed without taking the city. Such is the calamity of attacking cities.

Son Zi's comments have to be taken in context, because they come at the end of a passage advising that supreme importance should be given to achieving victory by means other than war, i.e. by disrupting alliances and the like, but nevertheless attacking cities comes last of all in the recommended courses of action for a wise general. Successive centuries were to prove Son Zi right, and walled towns and cities were comparatively safe if they were well prepared and stubbornly defended. Writing during the Warring States Period (550–221 BC) Mo Zi set out the classic exposition of the principles that lay behind good town defence in a state of siege:

> The city walls are to be high and thick; the ditch and moat are to be wide and deep; the towers are to be in good repair; the defensive weapons are to be mended and sharp; the firewood and food are to be sufficient to hold out for more than three months; the men are to be numerous and well chosen; the officers and people are to be in harmony; the important subjects who have

merit and long service with their superiors are to be many; the ruler is to be trustworthy and in the right; and the myriad people are to take pleasure in him.

These principles of preparation and cooperation were to hold good for many centuries of Chinese siege warfare and attacks on fortified cities by crossbow, catapult and ultimately cannon. Indeed it was often so difficult to take a town or city by force that attempts were made to negotiate surrender before any shots were fired. In some cases long discussions took place between the two competing generals. The biographer of Lu Zhonglian noted that 'He was able to devise cunning phrases to lift the siege of a beleaguered city'.

Yet cities were there to shelter people, and people needed feeding. Although the towns and cities of medieval China were more highly populated than contemporary European ones, starvation could be kept at bay if the city fathers had done their job properly and made sure that the granaries were well stocked. If a scorched earth policy had also been followed, then dwindling supplies of food and, crucially, fuel would have been more of a problem for the besiegers than to the besieged. The attacking enemy may well have plundered the countryside around, but when those supplies were exhausted he was forced to abandon the siege and move on unless his supplies could be replenished by an efficient transport system, which was often sadly lacking.

This drastic means of clearing the countryside and bringing the civilian population inside the walls would involve the wholesale destruction of valuable villages and farms, but an attempt was always made to take into the city anything that might be of use to the defenders to help their war effort and to deny it to the enemy. Lists exist from the time of the Song dynasty onwards of essential items to be brought within the walls and stockpiled. Apart from

This beautifully restored wooden tower stands over the northern gateway of Pingyao.

This is but one small section of the western wall of Pingyao, China's finest surviving fortified city. 'Horse-faced towers' with two-storey guardhouses above them protrude from the wall at regular intervals.

obvious items such as food supplies and fodder for horses, wood and bamboo, stones, copper, tiles and straw should be collected. From the time when firearms became more common materials such as sulphur, saltpetre, lead and iron were included. One source distinguishes between materials to be supplied for siege use from public stores and what is to be requisitioned from the civilian population. The exhaustive list for the former includes lamps and oil, axes, nitre, charcoal, sulphur, guns and cannon, bullets and shot, wooden gun carriages and mounts, broken tiles and stones, lime, wooden rafters, wooden boards, nails, needles, halberds and hooks. The latter category includes mats, hemp, bows, arrows, food, iron shovels, pestles, fuel, stones used for dressing textiles, straw, buckets for night soil, paper and water jars, ink and writing tables, wooden clubs and sticks. Buddhist and Daoist temples could become temporary granaries and storehouses. The empty spaces of a town therefore began to resemble a lumber yard, with stacks of firewood separated from piles of stout beams that could be used for making trebuchets. They were plastered over with mud to make them fire resistant against incendiary attacks, or, in the case of the trebuchet beams, kept in water. Workshops located in the outer suburbs were evacuated while markets and shops beyond the walls were suspended until the end of hostilities. A failure to comply with any of these requirements would incur a severe penalty – a deterrent that also applied to anyone who attempted to stockpile food in secret so as to speculate for his own profit.

If these measures were carried out to the letter, the approaching enemy would find a countryside that was deserted and denuded of all produce and assets for a wide area around the city. Even wells and water courses might be poisoned, although this was a risky strategy. Within the city its existing garrison would be augmented by the conscription of civilians. Able-bodied men would fight; women could be used for impressed labour, and even the weak could be of some use for carrying food or fuel. Anyone with a particular skill would be identified and used appropriately. Thus prepared, a city's inhabitants waited for the attack to come, trusting most of all in the sturdy walls that surrounded them.

THE GREAT FORTIFIED CITIES OF CHINA

As noted earlier, the greatest examples of fortified cities are naturally those that were used as dynastic capitals. The finest ones are described in the section that follows, along with two other examples chosen for their state of preservation and the consequent light they shine on Chinese fortifications.

Zhengzhou: the ancient walled city

The walls of the Shang capitals such as Zhenghou were of rammed earth. The base of the wall was between 10 and 20m wide, tapering upwards, and on either side of the wall were scarps of rammed earth. Each side of the city wall would have had between one and three gates, as we know from the excavated example at Yanshishang where the western gate was an earth and timber structure 2m wide and 16m long. There may well have been a reinforced gate tower on top and a row of timbers along the top of the wall. A moat 16m wide at the ground level and 6m at the bottom surrounded the walls.

Chang'an: the model capital

The great Ming dynasty walls of Xi'an, which so impress tourists as they head out of town to see the terracotta army, are mere youngsters when compared to the fortifications they replaced. Xianyang, the capital of the Qin dynasty, was the first fortified city to be located in the area around Xi'an. Its successor, the Western Han capital of Chang'an (Eternal Peace), was one and a half times the size of Rome, its contemporary lying at the other end of the Silk Road, but the Tang capital, also called Chang'an, was the most magnificent of all. Tang Chang'an was abandoned with the fall of the dynasty in AD 907, and no future dynasty ever set up its capital at Xi'an. However, during the early Ming dynasty the site was selected for a provincial capital and Xi'an (Western Peace) came into being.

Chang'an of the Tang had a remarkable symmetry on a north–south orientation. The huge rammed earth walls formed a nearly square shape, with a 155m-wide principal avenue running south from the palace *cheng* through the imperial *cheng* and on to the Mingdemen, the great southern gateway. As this road was reserved for sole use by the emperor and his processions, we may imagine with what awe a visiting ambassador might be struck on being conducted along this thoroughfare. It was to be a compliment paid in great sincerity by the copying of Tang Chang'an's designs for the capital cities of

The fortified harbour of Penglai (formerly Dengzhou) is currently being restored. It was built by the Ming as part of their 'Great Wall of the Sea' against the depredations of the *wako*. This view is taken from Penglai Pavilion. Note the two separate sections of Inner and Outer Harbour. The massive land gate appears in the distance.

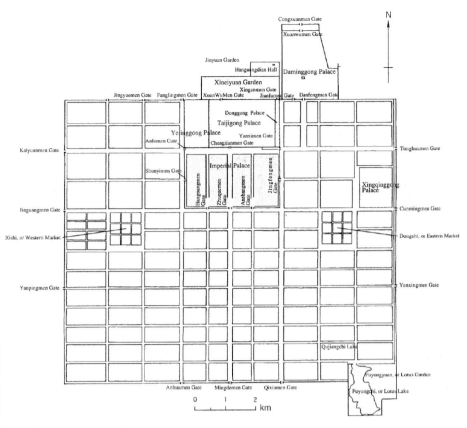

A plan of the layout of Chang'an (Xian), capital of the Tang dynasty. It was first built by the Sui dynasty and captured from them in AD 617. Visiting envoys would have been escorted into the magnificent city by the southern gate known as the Mingdemen. Chang'an was to provide the model for two successive Japanese capital cities. (After Ishihara Heizo)

neighbouring countries, most notably Heijo-kyo (Nara) in Japan and Heian-kyo (Kyoto) that succeeded Nara, both of which were miniature versions of Chang'an. The rest of the city was divided into *fang* (wards) within which strict social control was exercised, as described later. In AD 634 the strict symmetry of the place was broken when the emperor constructed a trapezoidal palace complex called Daming Gong, its shape determined more by the mundane concern about flooding and the need for higher ground than any fears about feng shui.

The Taijigong palace *cheng* of Chang'an, the capital of the Tang dynasty established where modern Xi'an now lies. This is a small section from an enormous illuminated model of Tang Chang'an on display in the museum in the Tang Paradise theme park in Xi'an. The Xuanwu Gate, site of the incident in AD 626 (see page 53), is identified in the bottom right-hand corner.

Xi'an of the Ming dynasty was located across only one-sixth of the area of former Chang'an, as is demonstrated by the fact that the two Wild Goose Pagodas are located outside the Ming walls. Yet even though Ming Xi'an was smaller in area, the walls that surrounded it were much more massive, its two major intersecting streets meeting at a splendid bell tower built in AD 1582.

Kaifeng: the fortress on the Yellow River

Kaifeng is located amid the alluvial plains of the Yellow River some 70km east of Zhengzhou. Like Zhengzhou it was a Shang settlement, and served as the capital for several minor dynasties until experiencing its heyday with the Song dynasty. Over the centuries Kaifeng suffered as much from flooding as from human invaders, the latter including the Jin who captured it in AD 1127 and lost it themselves to the Mongols after an epic siege in AD 1232. The shape of the walls is that of a square twisted slightly into a rhombus. Some sections of the wall have survived, and show more clearly than almost anywhere else the details of wall building that used rammed earth in successive layers, because the walls of Kaifeng are covered with brick only on their outer surfaces. Inside the walls the *hangtu* construction is revealed.

Two simple models of the city as it was under the Song are displayed in the city museum. One shows the whole Song city, the other the palatial *cheng* known as Dongting. The vibrant daily life of Kaifeng under the Song was captured for all time in the famous contemporary Qingming Scroll, although both its date and the identification of the city depicted as Kaifeng have been challenged. Yet this lively daily life was to end with the capture of the city by the Jin, who arrived under the walls of Kaifeng in December AD 1126. The city was badly denuded of troops, because armies had been dispatched to defend the various Song territories that were under threat. Peace talks were of no avail, and the wealthy citizens sent their valuables over the wall in an attempt to buy off the enemy, while the poor raided the imperial gardens for food and fuel. On 9 January AD 1127 the Jin took advantage of a considerable fall of snow to overwhelm the walls using three siege towers. It was an expensive victory, because the Jin lost 3,000 men compared to the defenders' 300, but when the Jin poured in to the city the struggle was abandoned and Emperor Qinzong hurried to satisfy the greed of the plunderers. Over a century later the victorious Jin were to feel similar despair when they in turn lost Kaifeng to the Mongols.

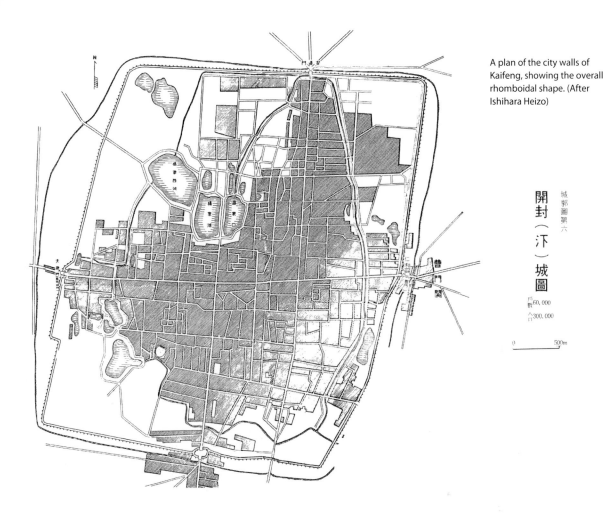

A plan of the city walls of Kaifeng, showing the overall rhomboidal shape. (After Ishihara Heizo)

城郭圖第六

開封（汴）城圖

比例60,000
人口300,000

0   500m

Beijing: the capital of the north

Very little now remains of the mighty walls that once enclosed Beijing, a city that was to provide the site for the capitals of several dynasties in or around the modern metropolis. The Liao dynasty made use of the site during the 10th century, calling it Nanjing or Yanjing. To the Jin it was Zhongdu, but it

The area outside the southern gate of Pingyao is currently being landscaped, and the extent of the clearance brings out the imposing nature of the bare walls. The solitary motor car provides an indication of scale.

The inner palace *cheng* of Yuan dynasty Dadu (Beijing) in AD 1300

This is an old photograph of the Yongdingmen, the southernmost gate in the outer wall of Beijing, which no longer exists. From here the visitor would travel north to the Qianmen.

was with the Mongol Yuan dynasty that Beijing came into its own as the capital of an empire. There was a certain irony in this, as the Mongols who had conquered China and much of central Asia had their domestic origins in felt tents, yet the Yuan dynasty's Dadu (the great capital) as they named it was as classical a model of imperial city as any that had gone before it. Rammed earth walls some 28.6km around framed a model of neat orientation of intersecting streets, its main difference from Chang'an being the location of the palace *cheng* to the south of the city's market.

The Ming dynasty, who overthrew the Yuan, chose Nanjing as their first capital, and the controversial move to Beijing required a great deal of rebuilding to take place. The Yongle Emperor who made the decision was quite convinced about the city's location, deeming it to be 'strong and secure. The mountains and rivers protect it well, and ten thousand nations lie on its four sides. It is a place favoured for sound reasons, by the mind of heaven and by exact divination.'

At the heart of the Yongle Emperor's vision lay the vast palace complex known to all as the Forbidden City, connected by an avenue to a majestic complex gate structure at the south called Zhengyangmen (the gate that faces directly to the sun) or Qianmen. During the 16th century an outer wall was added, and when the Qing dynasty took over Beijing, with no destruction of its architecture, this subdivision of the city provided the basis for a concentration of Manchu people within the inner city, known to European visitors as the 'Tartar city', and the banishment of Han Chinese to the 'Chinese city' outside.

C   THE INNER PALACE *CHENG* OF YUAN DYNASTY DADU (BEIJING) IN AD 1300

For all their origins as a nation who dwelt in felt tents, the Yuan (Mongol) emperors of China raised on the site of Beijing a fortified capital city that was fully within the established traditions of Chinese wall building and city planning. It was known as Dadu. In this plate we are looking into the inner palace *cheng* of the Yuan emperor. There is an extensive use of space in and around the magnificent palace which takes in two ornamental lakes, and a design of rectangular courtyards and city wards. The defensive walls are high and forbidding, yet possess a great delicacy and beauty. The one compromise with their steppe origins is the presence of *gers* (Mongol tents) in one outer courtyard.

The Qianmen or Zhengyangmen gate complex of Beijing originally consisted of two main gate towers joined together by a semicircular wall. Nowadays only the two gate towers remain. Here we are looking northwards from inside the archway of the outer gate towards the inner gate tower. Beyond that lies the Chairman Mao Mausoleum and the bleak Tian'anmen Square, which together ruin the original concept of a grand avenue stretching right up to the Forbidden City.

From AD 1533 onwards a visitor approaching Beijing from the south would first encounter the Yongdingmen in the southern wall of the Outer City. Passing through he would head north along an avenue that separated the walled Temple of Heaven in the east from the Temple of Mountains and Rivers to the west. After crossing the Tianqiao (Heavenly Bridge) the road narrowed as it approached the complex fortified structure of the Zhengyangmen. Nowadays it presents the appearance of two unconnected towers, but once a semicircular wall like a barbican, through which were three passages, joined the two together. The central entrance was used only by the emperor, and it was from Zhengyangmen that the Ghongzhen Emperor bade farewell to Li Jiantai, the Secretary of the Grand Council who set out with an army to quell the uprising of the rebel leader Li Zicheng. Two months later Li Zicheng conquered Beijing and overthrew the Ming dynasty, and thus unintentionally left the way open for the Manchu conquest.

Today's tourist then passes through the Qianmen complex and walks round the Chairman Mao Memorial Hall into the vast and bleak Tian'anmen Square. Until quite recently in history this was a more restricted area crossed by the imperial way as it passed north to the Tian'anmen (gate of heavenly peace) which originally dates from AD 1420 and towers 33.7m above the entrance to the Forbidden City. But there are still two gates to cross, the Duanmen and the Wumen, before the Forbidden City is reached.

Nanjing: the fortress on the Yangzi

Nanjing, better known in the West under its former Romanization as Nanking, is one of China's greatest cities. Its very name, which means 'southern capital', sets it against the 'northern capital' of Beijing. There are many differences between the two, not least of which is the topographical setting of Nanjing,

This model of Nanjing is displayed in the museum located within the Zhonghuamen gate complex. Although no attempt has been made to present the key buildings to scale with the walls, their relation to the curved design of Nanjing's city walls is clearly illustrated. The site of Jiankang, besieged in AD 548, occupied a small area at the central intersection of the roads. In the north-east is the Xuanwu Lake, and in the north-west is the Yangzi River.

which is dominated by its strategic proximity to the Yangzi River, and the presence of hills and lakes. This has ensured that it was only in the times when Nanjing was the capital of minor southern dynasties that it was surrounded by a square wall. The later Ming defences instead make use of the geography round about, soaring over hills and along river banks.

Nanjing received its first defences around 600 BC. By the time of the end of the Han dynasty it had been capital to several small states that employed the Yangzi as a natural moat. The epic siege of the city of Jiankang, which occupied a small square within the layout of modern Nanjing between AD 548 and AD 549, will be described later. Forty years later it fell to the Sui when they reunified China in AD 589. The building of the Grand Canal

Two visitors show the scale of this arched gateway through the walls of Nanjing.

followed, which added so much to the city's prosperity that it was to rival nearby Hangzhou, and when the Ming triumphed over the Yuan Nanjing became their first imperial capital.

The defence works for Nanjing that the new dynasty proposed took careful note of the complex topography on which the city lay. Fundamental to this was, of course, its position with regard to the Yangzi River and the small Qinhuai River, which flowed into the Yangzi around high ground in the north-west and acted as a natural moat on its western and southern sides. The walls on these sides were naturally made to follow the course of the Qinhuai River. To the north was another natural defence in the form of the Xuanwu Lake, a feature that had been made into an offensive weapon for flooding the city during the siege of AD 548–49. To the east, protected by excavated moats and ponds, the walls fringed the mountains of Xijin Shan. As the accompanying illustration of a model of Nanjing shows very clearly, the city walls, which total 32km in length, followed a highly irregular shape within these geographical constraints. In this way the design of Nanjing's fortifications differed considerably from that of Ming Beijing or Xi'an.

When the erstwhile rebel Zhu Yuan Zhang captured Nanjing in AD 1356 he acquired a modestly fortified city that included within it a former palace *cheng* of the Southern Song dynasty. The new walls were built between AD 1366 and AD 1386, although much of the city was complete by AD 1373. Within the vast curving outer wall the layout of the city presented certain aspects that would have been more familiar to visitors accustomed to the regular shapes of Beijing or Xi'an, because the imperial *cheng* in the east was

The Zhonghuamen is the finest single example of a fortified gateway to survive in China. \We are standing on the outer section, yet to be restored, which gives access to the bridge across the Qinhuai River. The sheer scale of the successive courtyards and the access ramp on the right is most impressive.

almost square. The city proper to the west of the imperial palace included surviving structures from earlier capitals. Zhu ordered 20,000 wealthy families to relocate there. To the north-west was a considerable open space, where the high ground provided a vantage point over the area where the Qinhuai entered the Yangzi.

Nanjing's impressive Ming walls were built on stone foundations, partly because much of the area round about was swampy or low-lying. The foundation stones and the bricks that constituted much of the outer and inner surfaces were brought to the site by river transport from numerous brickyards located round about. Quality control was established by requiring that each brick was stamped with the date and place of manufacture and the name of the maker. If any bricks were of insufficient quality they had to be replaced. The result was a wall whose gigantic serpentine nature made it resemble the Great Wall far more than its equally strong but rigidly straight contemporary in Xi'an.

Nanjing originally had 13 gates, but this eventually grew to 18, none of which were orientated to the cardinal directions but followed the natural curve of the river or the land. They included several major *wengcheng* (complex gate structures), of which outstanding surviving examples are the Zhongshanmen in the east and the most impressive great southern gate of the Zhubaomen, or Zhonghuamen as it became known during the 20th century. Few other places in China illustrate as well as this the castle-like nature of the finest Chinese city gates. Opening on to the Qinhuai River, when seen from this angle it is impressive only in terms of its bulk, which is a rectangular structure 118.5m wide and 21.5m high topped with battlements. It is only when one crosses the river bridge and enters the dark and heavily gated tunnel that its true scale becomes apparent, because it is pierced with tunnels and dark rooms. Yet one must now pass through no fewer than three more gated areas before entering the city, necessitating a total walk of about 1.5km. Each of these three inner gates had impressive towers, destroyed by the Japanese and recently restored. It is probably only a matter of time before the remaining gate tower over the first and most massive gate is also rebuilt. No less impressive are the two ramps that flank the gate complex to give access to the walls from inside the city.

Suzhou: the city on water

Suzhou, which dates from 514 BC when it was the capital of the State of Wu in the Spring and Autumn Period, possesses a unique water gate and canal defences round the Panmen at the south-western corner of the old city. The gate was rebuilt in AD 1351 and renovated under the Ming. Here the Grand Canal swings east, its waters joining up with those from the sluices of the double gateway system. The Panmen is actually a combination of a land gate and a water gate. The water gate is divided into two sections, each made of granite. The inner gate was originally equipped with a water sluice and a railed barrier. The outer gate has a width of 7.9m, a height of 7.8m and a depth of 3.9m. The inner gate is 8.9m high, 5.3m wide and 12.3m deep. Both openings are wide enough to allow two boats to pass through. Four large stone columns stand on a platform of layered bricks supporting an arched roof. The land gate is also of two sections.

Pingyao: the great survivor

Few places in the world deserve the title of 'unique', but this adjective can certainly be applied to the fortified city of Pingyao, China's great survivor.

The Panmen at Suzhou is a unique gate complex consisting of a land gate and a water gate, topped with an ornate gate tower.

Located approximately 90km south of Taiyuan, Pingyao owes its survival partly to chance and partly to a flood in 1977 where the walls acted as a levee and saved the city. This may have concentrated the minds of the citizens when proposals were put forward in 1981 to modernize Pingyao, a process that elsewhere had involved the construction of wide roads and a deliberate attempt to open up walled areas to the countryside. Some parts of the wall had

Because it follows the course of a small river the southern wall of Pingyao is the only one to possess a curve. It is also the most isolated section of the *cheng*.

D THE FORTIFIED CITY OF PINGYAO AS A SYMBOLIC TORTOISE, C. AD 1560

The miraculously preserved fortified city of Pingyao is the finest extant example of a Ming walled city. The overall shape is supposed to represent a tortoise, the symbol of longevity. The four gates at the east and west are supposed to be the tortoise's legs. The southern gate, which leads directly to a water source, is its head, while the northern gate, situated in a low-lying area through which rainwater and sewage is drained, is the tail and anus. Two wells outside the southern gate symbolize its eyes. The north-east gate is said to be symbolically tied to the Lutai Pagoda to the north-east of the city so that the tortoise would not escape. Around its perimeter are 3,000 battlements and 72 horse-face towers; these are said to represent the 72 saints of Confucius and his 3,000 disciples. The southern wall, which follows a river, is the only one that is curved. In the centre of the city the two main thoroughfares almost meet at a fine tower.

The fortified city of Pingyao as a symbolic tortoise c. AD 1560

already fallen down, and others were indeed demolished, but not sufficiently for the overall plan to be positively thwarted. Restoration began in 1980, and in 1997 Pingyao was declared a UNESCO World Heritage Site. Since then all urban development has taken place outside the old walled city, producing an urban landscape that is drearily familiar, and a warning of what might have been. Nowadays demolition of a new kind is taking place, and during my visit in 2007 I was intrigued to see the extent of the landscaping that is taking place immediately outside the walls, leaving a barren glacis in front of a wall that must now look very much as it did during the Ming dynasty.

It is in fact to the Ming dynasty that Pingyao owes its present appearance, when contemporary methods of wall construction were used to improve and expand what already existed from the time of the Northern Wei. This was AD 1370, when Pingyao was designated using the accepted hierarchy for cities as 'a city of three li'. So the walls were each three li long apart from the southern wall, which is not straight but follows the Zhongdu River so that the three li measures the distance between the corner towers as the crow flies. Its curve is quite noticeable if one walks round the outside. The southern wall is the most deserted section, while the West Gate is surrounded by traffic.

The wall of Pingyao is almost square with a total perimeter of 6.2km and ringed with a moat. It is about 10m high, 9 to 12m wide at the base and 3 to 6m wide at the top, where it is paved with greenish coloured bricks. There is a pronounced slope down into the city. The walkway on the wall is well drained so that rain will not damage the wall, and water is conducted into the city through stone spouts.

On the outer rim of the wall are battlements each 2m high, with a smaller safety parapet on the inner side 0.6m high. Each battlement possesses an additional loophole. Every 40 or 100m along the wall is a protruding tower called a *mamian* (horse face) which allows flanking fire. The crenellations are continued round the tower and each horse-face tower has a two-storey

The tower at the corner intersection of the northern and western walls of Pingyao under floodlights.

This delicate corner tower stands at the intersection of the northern and eastern walls of Pingyao.

guardroom rising up from the parapet reminiscent of the towers on the Great Wall. They were used for weapon storage and signalling. There are six gates in all, two on each of the east and west walls, and one on each of the southern and northern walls. Each gate is a *wencheng* with a narrow but steep courtyard that is very forbidding, and is entered by a dark archway. The outer barbican is in each case very large. On top of each gate is a gate tower, superbly restored. There used to be a large wooden watchtower at each corner, but only one has so far been reconstructed.

The overall layout of Pingyao is also interesting because of its symbolism. Its 3,000 battlements and 72 horse-face towers are said to represent the 72 saints of Confucius and his 3,000 disciples. The overall shape is supposed

The northern wall of Pingyao as seen from a vantage point on the inside of the western wall. Its height is most impressive. Note the small parapet on the inner side and the pronounced slope. The northern gate tower stands out in the setting sun.

to represent a tortoise, the symbol of longevity. The four gates at the east and west are supposed to be the tortoise's legs. The southern gate, which leads directly to a water source, is its head, while the northern gate, situated in a low-lying area through which rainwater and sewage is drained, is the tail and anus. Two wells outside the southern gate symbolize its eyes. The north-east gate is said to be symbolically tied to the Lutai Pagoda to the north-east of the city – so that the tortoise would not escape!

Zhang Bi: a fortified city in miniature

Out of all the survivors of the thousands of fortified towns and cities that once dotted the Chinese countryside few are more fascinating than tiny Zhang Bi in Shanxi province, which lies 10km south-east of Jiexiu. Perfectly preserved and recently restored, Zhang Bi is like a fortified city in miniature where small details of fortifications, often absent from larger examples, may be readily studied. Yet the size of Zhang Bi makes it something of a mystery. Is it a fortified village, or an actual fortress that challenges the conventional notion that there is no such thing as a Chinese castle? The closest European analogy would be with the hilltop villages of Provence in France, or a crusader castle site where houses were built within the walls.

Zhang Bi is believed to have been built originally by Liu Wuzhou around the time of the founding of the Tang dynasty. Liu Wuzhou was one of the rebel leaders associated with the fall of the Sui dynasty. In AD 617 he murdered the governor of Mayi Commandery to the south-west of Datong, opened the granaries, brought the surrounding area under his own control and took an imperial title. He was eventually defeated by Li Shimin, the future Tang Emperor Taizong, and Zhang Bi remains his only memorial. In fact the inhabitants of Zhang Bi constructed the Kehan Memorial Temple for him, which still stands within the village and houses statues of Liu Wuzhou and his two loyal followers.

There is no rectangular layout to Zhang Bi. Instead the village is a long S-shape that has been likened to that of a dragon, a design that derives simply from Zhang Bi's extraordinary position on a dry, rocky bluff 1,000m above sea level along precipitous cliffs. Before describing the village itself, we may note that the cliffs are pierced by a long, winding tunnel. It is entered from the village and emerges in the cliff face overlooking a steep-sided gorge.

This view of the northern gateway of Pingyao illustrates the *wengcheng* principle whereby the gate is entered at 90 degrees from the passage through into the city.

38

The whole tunnel is 5km long and winds in an S-shape over three layers. The upper tunnel lies between one and two metres from the surface; the middle tunnel is 8–10m down, while the lowest level descends to 17 or 20m. Only one person can pass at a time. It possesses caves for stationing as many as 20 troops as well as underground stables. There are vantage points and drainage systems. To aid ventilation the tunnel is connected to ten wells sunk from the village, and at the lowest level are underground grain storage facilities.

Zhang Bi is no less remarkable above ground. There are only two gates. The North Gate is brick built and fronts onto the gorge, while the southern gate, which is smaller and built around a stone arch provided the most practical

A sentry stands guard outside the northern gate of Pingyao, from where the wall continues round.

Zhang Bi provides an unusual example of a fortified village. Dating from the time of the Tang dynasty, it is like a fortified city in miniature. Being built on a bluff its defences make use of a series of tunnels that lead down from the village and come out here above the gorge. Part of the walls may be seen in the top left.

entrance. Both are remarkably well defended. Just inside the southern gate is a large ramp giving access to the walls, but it is at the northern end of the village where its fortress nature is most apparent. Here neat brickwork battlements surmount a complex *wengcheng* involving a 90-degree turn through an exposed courtyard. Between the two gates lies a delightful collection of low-rise buildings including temples and shrines.

THE LIVING SITES

The fortified city at peace

In Ancient China the peasants had to stay in their hamlets while their lords and their followers lived within the *cheng*, but in the absence of town charters or even a code of civil law the citizens of a fortified town or city enjoyed little civic liberty, nor would the scholar-officials who ruled the roost tolerate any form of private enterprise. Towns did not therefore become a magnet for the population as in the West. Rebels chose to take refuge in villages, and we frequently hear of a rebellion beginning with an attack on a town, rather than rising within the town itself.

Within the city or town the lives of its inhabitants were – theoretically at least – strictly controlled, a matter given physical expression in the medieval period when the insides of towns and cities were squared off into the wards called *fang*, which were then subdivided into alleyways. These wards could be closed off at night for security. Until AD 636 the ward gates of Tang Chang'an were opened at dawn to the shouts of the military patrols. Centres of officialdom were separated from the lower orders by further walls, and the Tang Penal Code promised 75 blows for trespassing on ramparts, the inner enclosures or even the low walls separating the wards. But towards the end of the Tang dynasty the expansion of trade and consequent increase in population made it impossible to divide up the inhabitants as they had once been. There was consequently much

---

E   **THE TRIPLE SOUTHERN GATE OF NANJING, AD 1587**

The Zhonghuamen, the southern gate of Nanjing, is the finest, and probably the largest, example of a fortified gate complex in China. Opening on to the Qinhuai River, when seen from this angle it is impressive only in terms of its bulk, which is a rectangular structure 118.5m wide and 21.5m high topped with battlements. It is only when one crosses the river bridge and enters the dark tunnel that its true scale becomes apparent, because it is pierced with tunnels and dark rooms. Yet one must now pass through no less than three more gated areas before entering the city, necessitating a total walk of about 1.5km. Each of these three inner gates had impressive towers, destroyed by the Japanese and recently restored. No less impressive are the two ramps that flank the gate complex to give access to the walls from inside the city.

The triple southern gate of Nanjing, AD 1587

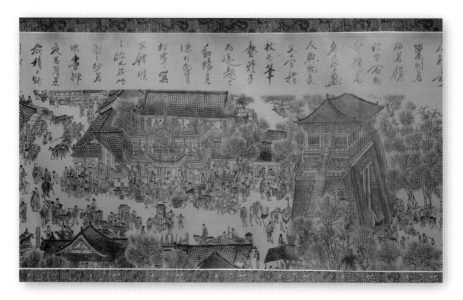

more freedom of movement, and nocturnal markets were even held. Kaifeng in the 12th century and Hangzhou in the 13th (as so memorably described by Marco Polo) were very lively places where dwelt disreputable people such as actors, singers, prostitutes, jugglers and storytellers. Trade was conducted with a wide variety of food being sold and exotic goods being brought from afar.

The fortified city in times of war

When war loomed, the paternalism and social control that was applied to the civilian population in peacetime became even more intrusive. This was largely because it was taken for granted that the poorer members of society would pose the greatest problems of loyalty and service. Simply put, the poor would either run away or be a burden, and might even cooperate with a successful enemy by leading plunderers to the homes of the rich and looting their own share. One ancient authority is quoted as saying that if a town was besieged then one should first look to the interior situation and only then give consideration to the enemy dispositions.

In times of war the cities, having acted as permanent camps to house warriors, became also places of refuge: temporary strongholds for the entire agricultural population. A city may have had a double rampart but the fields extended right into the town, making evacuation of the countryside less of a problem than it might have been. Such a situation whereby everyone without exception had been hurriedly brought within the city walls allowed of course for the unwanted presence of spies and fifth columnists. Itinerant tradesmen and vagrants were particularly suspect in this regard. The preventative measures to be adopted included the issuing of identification tags and the control of access through designated gates manned by officials with a good memory for faces. Yet the most important means for weeding out spies was by the normal surveillance exercised by groups of ten families over their neighbours. Any innkeeper or even the abbot of a monastery found to have a suspicious person on his premises would be punished.

In general, the successful maintenance of civilian morale, law and food supplies during a siege situation required the complete opposite to the principle of carrying on as normal. Family parties and celebration were banned. Tight night-time curfews were imposed. Magicians and fortune tellers, who would be ideal targets for gossip and the planting of false rumours, were strictly controlled, as was any over-indulgence in alcohol that might cause tongues to be loosened.

As to the positive contribution that the beleaguered citizens might make to the war effort none was more important than the prevention, detection and extinguishing of fires. With many buildings made of wood with thatched roofs even an accidental fire during peacetime could be devastating. In Hangzhou in AD 1341 a fire destroyed 15,755 buildings with the loss of 74 lives and the making homeless of 10,797 families. In a siege situation whereby fire and explosives could be launched into a city by catapult, or even small incendiaries taken in by the ingenious use of birds, fire prevention was of the highest priority. Water supplies were usually limited during a siege, and might consist of little more than large jars placed on the streets. For this reason a civilian fire brigade was a necessity, and every city quarter was required to supply a crew of 40 fire fighters, whose duties were closely delineated. The first ten would use hooks to demolish the burning building and anything vulnerable adjacent to it to create a fire break. Ten more men filled the buckets, five carried the water and five more used the water to put the fire out. The remaining five patrolled the streets round about to guard against looting. Special precautions were taken in the case of gunpowder storage. Gunpowder was kept in earthenware jars covered in clay in holes dug into the earth near each city gate. The water stores near the gunpowder magazines were guarded by soldiers, and anyone approaching them was treated as potentially hostile.

The greatest fear of any defending general was that the siege would be so prolonged that his food supplies ran out before either a relieving army appeared or the besieging army abandoned the effort because of a similar shortage of food. At Fengtian in AD 783 men were lowered by ropes from the city walls by night to go scavenging because it was important that the garrison should be well fed and kept warm. For women and children it was sufficient just for them to avoid starvation, and in three extreme cases starving garrisons appear to have resorted to cannibalism. An emissary sent out to the besieging Chu forces around the Song capital in 593 BC during the Spring and Autumn Period

A fire in a city as the result of a siege appears in this painting in a temple in Pingyao. Fire was a constant preoccupation of the defenders of a besieged city.

reported that 'In the city we are exchanging our children and eating them, and splitting up their bones for fuel'. This of course may have been a falsehood to make the besiegers think that the city would never surrender, as may have been the serious charge of cannibalism laid at the door of a wicked anti-Sui rebel leader at the time of the founding of the Tang dynasty. He allegedly forced communities under his control to supply women and children with which to feed his troops, and was quite proud of the fact. 'As long as there are still people in the other states', he boasted, 'what have we to worry about?'

A much more reliable account of cannibalism concerns the siege of Suiyang in AD 757, where the heroic Zhang Xun, who was put to death when the city fell after a siege of ten months, is believed to have instituted cannibalism as a planned and organized response to starvation. The city had been low on supplies even when the siege began, and before long those sheltering within its walls had augmented their meagre grain supplies with paper, tree bark and tea leaves. When all the horses had been eaten the soldiers consumed all the rats and birds that they could catch, and when these ran out Zhang Xun ordered them to kill and eat the civilian population, beginning first with the women, and when there were no women left to eat old men and young boys. To set an example Zhang Xun, whose own wife and children were not inside the city, sacrificed his favourite concubine and made the soldiers eat her flesh. Had he managed to hold out for just a few days more using these appalling methods Suiyang would have been relieved by a fast approaching army, and subsequent events were to prove that Zhang Xun's desperate measures to defend Suiyang made an enormous contribution to the eventual Tang victory. Condemnation of Zhang Xun was therefore somewhat muted, and more sympathy was expressed for the men forced to eat human flesh than those who were unfortunate enough to be eaten.

Military personnel and the siege situation

A city's standing army would be preoccupied during peacetime with the tedious business of keeping watch from the battlements. Small considerations such as the supply of fruit and iced drinks during summer and the provision of umbrellas against the sun's heat made the task more bearable. In winter warm clothing and soup similarly kept morale at an acceptable level. Not surprisingly, during a siege their responsibilities became much more acute, and military discipline was enforced every bit as strictly as the control of the civilian population. For example, messages from the enemy sent as arrow letters were not to be opened but should be taken directly to the commanding officer, nor should anyone spontaneously sound a trumpet or raise a flag in case this should be a signal to the enemy. At the very least this would interfere with the precise orders given concerning the issuance of warnings of attack. These would come from observation towers on the wall or from detached forward lookout posts and consist of flags by day or cannon shots and lanterns by night. When such signals were spotted the order was given to reinforce the walls.

The military preparations that the garrison of a Chinese fortified city might take to be ready for a siege started long before the enemy actually came into sight and complemented the civilian measures. The first need was to block his access, particularly along roads, which might be sown with caltrops, four-pointed metal spikes arranged in a tetrahedron shape so that they always landed with one spike pointing upwards. This was done by the Jin when the Mongols approached Beijing in AD 1211. More sophisticated forms of roadblocks consisted of collapsible fences or traps, or old sword blades

Plan of the rammed earth city walls of Datong. Several sections still survive. (After Ishihara Heizo)

mounted on boards. A later version was called an 'earth stopper', a flat wooden board into which barbed nails were hammered. A more subtle device was the use of dummy soldiers made of straw and bedecked with flags, to make the enemy think that the garrison was much larger than it actually was.

When the enemy attacked, the garrison, of course, should always stand firm, and even during a fire soldiers were strictly forbidden to leave their posts on the walls. These posts were strictly defined by the number of men spread between the number of openings on the battlements, arranged in groups of five under a leader within larger unit lengths of 25 and 100, each subdivision being identified by a flag using a Chinese ideograph in an alphabetical arrangement. No one was allowed to move more than five paces from his post, and even a group leader who strayed into the adjacent set of battlements might be decapitated. Silence was everywhere enforced. Conversation had to be whispered, and people summoned by their officers just by waving a hand. The guard units would work an eight-hour shift on wall duty or even a 12-hour shift if numbers were restricted, but in a wall crew of five men four were permitted to sleep at night with one standing on sentry duty. Temporary shelters were built against the weather, but no one was allowed to leave his post to collect food. Instead two meals were brought up by carriers onto the walls every day between 07.00 and 09.00 and between 15.00 and 17.00. During enemy attacks food was hoisted up on to the walls using ropes.

Hand-held weapons such as axes, maces, hammers, halberds and flails were piled up and kept ready for destroying the enemy's scaling ladders. One large iron latrine bucket was supplied for every 25 men. During attacks the bucket would be heated and the contents ladled onto the heads of assault parties. Otherwise small stones would be dropped onto individual attackers and bigger boulders used to crush scaling ladders and other siege devices. Some stones might be tied by ropes so that they could be used again, but more common were the ingenious spiked cylinders that could be rolled down the outer surfaces

of the walls to clear them of attackers, or the massive spiked boards on chains that crushed opponents in a similar way. Yet on many occasions the defenders on a city wall had to face some formidable siege engines and ingenious siege techniques. These ranged from the mundane, such as ramming, mining and missile bombardment, to the bizarre use of herds of oxen to the tails of which were attached burning brands. Their use is recorded for the year 279 BC when Tian Dan, the general of the state of Qi, was besieged inside the city of Jimo. He is said to have broken the siege by taking a herd of 1,000 oxen, fitting sharp daggers on their horns and reeds soaked in oil to their tails and sending them off in the direction of the siege lines. Many years later at the siege of De'an in AD 1132 by the Jin, the Song defenders used a single fire ox to add to the impact of their sortie out of the city with fire lances.

Fire was also spread by more conventional means. *Pi li pao* were exploding fire bombs thrown by catapult. They had casings made from many layers of stiffened paper and were filled with gunpowder and pieces of broken porcelain or iron to inflict personal injury. A larger and clumsier version of a soft-case bomb bore a name that indicated that it was the match for 'ten thousand enemies'. The housing of the ten thousand enemies' bomb was of clay, and the whole was enclosed in a cuboid wooden framework or a wooden tub so that the missile did not break before its fuse detonated the explosive. The reason for this is that the ten thousand enemies was neither thrown by a rope sling nor projected from a trebuchet, but simply dropped over the battlements of a castle, and there is a well-known illustration showing how the resulting explosion could blow the besiegers to pieces. 'The force of the explosion spins the bomb round in all directions, but the city walls protect one's own men from its effects on that side, while the enemy's men and horses are not so fortunate,' says a passage dating from the end of the Ming dynasty.

Unlike the soft-casing thunderclap bombs, the *zhen tian lei* (thunder-crash bombs or, more literally 'heaven shaking thunder') killed people by the shattering of their metal cases and destroyed objects by the increased force of the explosion that is implied by the dramatically enhanced name. The introduction of thunder-crash bombs is credited to the Jin, and their first recorded use in war dates from the siege by the Jin of the Southern Song city of Qizhou in AD 1221. The list of siege weapons used at Qizhou by the besiegers was an eclectic mix of the primitive and the modern, ranging from Greek Fire projectors and expendable birds carrying small incendiaries, to these new exploding cast iron bombs. They were shaped like a bottle gourd with a small opening, and were made from cast iron about two inches thick. The fragments produced when the bombs exploded caused great personal injury, and one Southern Song officer was blinded in an explosion which wounded half a dozen other men.

There were of course occasions when an enemy would capture a section of the walls and fighting would begin in the streets, so this was taken into consideration in defence planning. If the city possessed an inner and an outer wall then the enemy could be trapped between the two. Pitfalls were dug and roadblocks set up, particularly on the approaches to sensitive areas such as gunpowder stores and granaries, as such places would be prime targets. One authority recommends that in the case of a sizeable incursion the civilians should be encouraged to flee the city. Booby traps could be arranged for the incoming enemy, as was done in AD 1277 when Guilin in Guangxi province, one of the last outposts of Southern Song resistance to the Mongols, lay under siege. When the main tower fell a truce was arranged so that the garrison could receive supplies prior to an honourable surrender. During the interregnum some Mongol soldiers climbed up on to the now undefended walls, when suddenly there was an enormous explosion which brought down the wall and the Mongols with it. The Southern Song defenders had prepared a huge bomb at its foundations, and had ignited it at just the right moment.

THE SITES AT WAR

Unlike the Great Wall of China, the fortified cities of China witnessed an extensive operational history over many centuries and many dynasties. I have selected the following case studies from the vast array of examples available for two reasons: first, because they illustrate the points made earlier about the correct military and civilian preparations to make when facing a siege. Second, in addition to defensive actions the examples also involve an interesting variety of besieging techniques spanning a time from the era of crossbows and catapults to the use of exploding bombs and cannon. The devices themselves are covered in detail in my *Siege Weapons of the Far East* books available from Osprey Publishing.

Yubi, AD 546

In the account of the siege of Yubi in AD 546 every conventional means of assault seems to have been employed during Gao Huan of the Eastern Wei's second unsuccessful attempt to take the city, which was surrounded by fine walls made of rammed earth. The first siege had ended after nine days when a blizzard claimed the lives of many of Gao Huan's soldiers as they stood exposed before the city. The second siege lasted approximately 50 days, and on taking up his new positions Gao Huan began operations by cutting off the city's water supply and then ordering a huge earth and wood mound to be constructed against the south wall. It eventually grew so large as to challenge the advantage of height possessed by the defenders on the wall and even in the two towers that surmounted it. The city's commander. Wei Xiaokuan.

The Qianmen gate complex of Beijing in the late Ming dynasty under attack from the Manchus in AD 1644

A siege scene from a bas relief in the National Military Museum, Beijing. We see the use of battering rams against the gates, scaling ladders and cannon.

responded by increasing the height of the towers using timber, a feat that Gao Huan could not match. Acknowledging defeat on this score, Gao Huan announced that he would bore a hole through the wall instead. Ten tunnels in all were dug, to which the defenders responded by countermining, not for each individual tunnel but by digging a long tunnel parallel to the southern wall and thus perpendicular to any hostile mine that might be discovered. But even though the first men out of it might quickly be killed, once a tunnel had broken through into the city it could remain potentially dangerous as a hidden pathway that was still open for use at a future time. The defenders therefore placed piles of combustible materials on the surface of the ground along their defensive trench. In case of need these piles could quickly be pushed into the trench and ignited. Great bellows were then used to force the flames and smoke into the tunnel and against the faces of Gao Huan's men within. In view of the fact that Gao Huan's ten tunnels may have been distributed over a wide distance, it is clear that an adequate defence would require either a very large number of men or some means of guessing at what particular spot a threat was to be expected. The defenders on top of the south wall and its two towers might spot concentrations of men entering one or another tunnel, but such visual intelligence would disappear at night or behind natural or artificial cover. They may therefore have used some form of listening device as will be described later for the siege of De'an.

F   **THE QIANMEN GATE COMPLEX OF BEIJING IN THE LATE MING DYNASTY UNDER ATTACK FROM THE MANCHUS IN AD 1644**

The complex fortified structure of the Zhengyangmen or Qianmen in Beijing is shown here as it was at the time of the fall of the Ming dynasty. Nowadays it presents the appearance of two unconnected towers, but once a semicircular wall joined the two together. The central entrance was used only by the emperor, but there were also two side entrances, each defended by a barbican. Here fairs and markets were held in time of peace. The outer tower, substantially rebuilt in recent times, was known as the Gate Tower, while the inner tower was called the Arrow Tower. As at Nanjing, they are solidly built from brick and stone around a rammed earth core.

Gao Yuan next tried to breach the south wall by breaking it with a battering ram under the cover of a wagon. This initially had great effect, because the defenders at first found nothing with which they could stop the assault wagon. Wei Xiaokuan eventually ordered the manufacture of large curtains from sheets of cloth sewn together. His men suspended the curtains from long poles which they manipulated from the battlements. Soon they were then able to anticipate the intended target of the ram and deftly dropped their curtain down between target and ram to absorb its impact. Gao Huan tried to burn the curtains using long torches of oil-soaked tinder bound to bamboo poles. These were in turn countered by long hooked staffs with which the men on top of the wall hacked at the torches and sent the burning tinder floating harmlessly down outside the wall. The curtains were saved, as were the towers.

Gao Huan had sought unsuccessfully to go over, to go under, and to go through the south wall. Now he sought to collapse the wall by sapping at its foundations. This was obviously a major push against Yubi, because these operations were carried on against all four faces of the city at 21 different locations. Each of the tunnels apparently branched off under the wall to create a sizeable intersection which Gao Huan then supported with oil-soaked props of wood. When the supports were ignited and burned, the section of wall lost its support and collapsed. Yet once again the resourceful Wei Xiaokuan was able to reply effectively even to this threat by quickly erecting palisades in front of every section of collapsed wall and thus keeping out the invaders. The rammed earth construction of the wall must have been sufficiently sturdy to minimize the length of wall which collapsed over each mine, thus giving him scope to do this.

In desperation Gao Huan turned to negotiation, both formally with the commander and informally with the troops he wished to seduce into his service. Arrow letters fell into the city bearing the message that anyone who beheaded the City Commander and surrendered Yubi would be honoured with high rank and rewarded with houses and many bolts of silk. Wei Xiaokuan took one of the leaflets and personally wrote on the back, 'If there be one who will behead Gao Huan, I will grant the same reward.' He then shot the leaflet back out over the city wall into the midst of the Eastern Wei attackers. Neither offer was taken up.

The streets of Pingyao looking towards the central tower which marks the intersection of its main thoroughfares.

Gao Huan's last stratagem of all was to behead, in full view of the city, Wei Xiaokuan's younger brother, whom he had somehow acquired, but Wei Xiaokuan still stood firm, and it became apparent that with this final act of desperation Gao Huan had exhausted both his arsenal of tactics and his reservoir of physical strength. Then one night a falling star was seen over the Eastern Wei camp. It caused terrified foreboding in Gao Huan's remaining forces. As if in fulfillment of the omen, Gao Huan fell sick, drained in both body and mind, and ordered the siege to be lifted. A withdrawal was carried under cover of night and the ordeal of Yubi came to an end. Gao Huan died only a few weeks later.

Jiankang, AD 548–49

Similar events occurred during another siege in southern China a couple of years later. This involved the rebellion of a frontier general called Hou Jing, who posed the most serious threat during the hegemony of the short-lived Liang dynasty, which lasted only 55 years. In AD 548 Hou Jing laid siege to their capital city Jiankang, which lay on the site of modern Nanjing on the Yangzi River. We read first of the population fleeing inside and causing panic as they raised the numbers within the city to many tens of thousands, and even the troops of the city garrison seem to have looked first to their own personal needs until a few officers were relieved of their heads as an example to the others. A regrettable delay in removing boats from the pontoon bridge across the river crossing, omitted simply to avoid causing dismay to the citizens, enabled the besiegers to gain the initiative.

The Sui capture of Jiankang (modern Nanjing) in AD 589 appears in this painting in the National Military Museum in Beijing. The victory was crucial to the Sui dynasty's control of the south of China, and stood in marked contrast to the short-lived triumph at Jiankang of Hou Jing in AD 549.

Hou Jing quickly replaced the dislodged pontoons, and fire was laid against three of the four city gates. The defenders extinguished the fires, so a minor gate was attacked by chopping at it with long-handled axes, but the defenders drilled holes into the gates and thrust long-shafted spears through the apertures into the chests of the demolition squads. Flat-roofed covered wagons were then brought up to protect men undermining the walls, but rocks smashed them, so they were replaced with ones with sharply pitched roofs. The defenders then dropped 'pheasant tail torches' on to them. These were simple incendiaries made of reed and grasses in a 'V' shape that were either ignited and then dropped onto the central ridge of the wagon roofs, or thrown down carefully and then set alight using fire arrows. This brought the current action to a halt, so Hou Jing constructed mobile siege towers of some sort, but their wheels sank into the soft ground.

The attack then settled down into an attempt at a blockade, with two very similar features to those noted earlier at Yubi. The first was the sending of messages into the city promising rewards for any traitors. The second occurred when the besiegers exhibited the commander's son whom they had captured, and threatened to kill him. The records tell us that to show his great resolve the commander loosed an arrow at the boy himself! Hou Jing was suitably impressed and let the boy go.

Hou Jing then detached a force to capture the nearby town of Dongfu, which was treacherously betrayed when some defenders allowed Hou Jing's men to sneak over the wall. The heads of the defenders of Dongfu were piled up within sight of the inhabitants of Jiankang to intimidate them, but still there was no surrender. Hou Jing then built earthen mounds on the east and west sides of the city, but the defenders successfully undermined them and raised mounds of their own inside the walls, so the besiegers abandoned the mounds and pulled back. Hou Jing then resorted to an attempt to flood the city by releasing the waters of the Xuanwu Lake, but even though there was an inundation the garrison stood firm.

The siege of Jiankang finally ended ignominiously after Hou Jing negotiated a spurious truce. During the absence of hostilities Hou Jing regrouped his army and then returned to Jiankang in greater force. Another deluge from the Xuanwu Lake followed, but the eventual fall of the city was caused by two traitors who opened the gates. Eighty percent of the inhabitants of the city had either succumbed to starvation of illness or had been killed during the fighting to give Hou Jing his victory. His triumph, however, was short lived, because after setting up and deposing two protégés he became emperor himself in AD 551, only to be driven out of Jiankang by Liang loyalists. He died as he was making his escape towards the sea.

Fengtian, AD 783

The Tang emperors and their splendid international city of Chang'an may have been the epitome of elegance, but the threat of warfare was never far away. In AD 783, for example, the Tang emperor Dezong fled from Chang'an in the face of a combination of mutinous soldiers and a rioting mob. The emperor took refuge in the walled city of Fengtian (modern Qian) 80km away, where he was joined by Hun Zhen, the man who was to play the greatest part in its defence. Another reinforcement arrived shortly afterwards. The rebels, under their leader Zhu Ci, tried to follow the army into the city, but were kept out by the use of wagons of burning straw.

There was therefore little opportunity for the defenders of Fengtian to put into operation the approved means of preparation of a siege, but nor did Zhu Ci have the leisure to prepare extensively for his attack. Realizing that he would now have to mount a siege against Fengtian, Zhu Ci hired the services of a Buddhist monk called Fa-jian who was skilled in siege weaponry. Fa-jian responded positively to his commission by demolishing a nearby Buddhist temple in order to obtain timber to build a cloud ladder. Judging by the precise words used to describe it and by indications given of its height, the device was probably a fixed wooden 'staircase on wheels' rather than the hinged and pivoted type of siege ladder that also goes under the same name. It must have been enormous because it was manhandled by 500 men, and Fa-jian took into consideration the fact that the wood used would be tinder-dry, so he wrapped it with wet felt and fresh animal hides and tied bags of water to its sides. As the vehicle inched forward it was shadowed on each side by covered assault wagons, underneath which were men carrying brushwood and soil with which to fill up the moat.

The time taken to build the machine gave the defenders ample opportunity to assess how to counter it. Two points emerged: first, its weight, and second, its flammability. In response to the first weakness a tunnel was dug parallel to the wall into which its wheels would be likely to sink. The tunnel was filled with horse dung to a depth of two metres, which would give off gases that could be ignited, and other combustible materials were piled up nearby. The defence plan worked perfectly, because one wheel crashed through the weakened ground into the tunnel and flames came out of the ground when the gases were ignited. More burning materials were then hurled down on to it from the walls.

Frustrated by this reversal Zhu Ci bombarded the city using multiple crossbows, but soon had to abandon the siege altogether when a relieving army arrived and rescued the Tang emperor after a month of privation.

Xiangyang and De'an, AD 1206–07

Yubi, Jiankang and Fengtian may have illustrated a wide range of stratagems concerning an attack on a fortified city, but our next examples provide a classic application of the accepted means of defence. Reference was previously made to the celebrated siege of Xiangyang by the Mongols between AD 1268 and 1273 and the decisive use of counterweight trebuchets. Yet this was not the first time this strategic city had come under siege, because in AD 1206 it provided a focus for the rivalry between the Jin and the Southern Song in an epic siege that lasted 90 days. The siege of De'an to the south-east of Xiangyang lasted two weeks longer and was another aspect of the Jin's drive against the Song in their attempt to reach the Yangzi River.

Huang Chao's peasant army attack Chang'an in AD 881 in this painting in the National Military Museum, Beijing. The Tang emperor fled, but Huang Chao's assumption of the imperial title was not acknowledged beyond the city walls, and he was harried to his death three years later.

Yue Fei was a general of the Southern Song who led the fight back against the Jin. In AD 1140 he took up siege positions outside Kaifeng in an attempt to recapture the Song's ancient capital. Political intrigue, however, led to his recall and martyrdom. This wall painting is in the temple to Yue Fei in Hangzhou and depicts him outside Kaifeng.

Xiangyang lay directly on the Han River with walls leading down to its banks. These fortifications were reinforced using wooden palisades and the remains of carts and carriages. Being heavily outnumbered, the garrison had followed established practice and augmented their armed forces by training local civilians, among whom many were associated with the tea trade. As tea was a state monopoly smuggling was rife, so bodyguards were regularly employed by the tea merchants, and these toughs made excellent auxiliaries in times of war. The other recommendation noted earlier that the surrounding countryside should be cleared was also followed. In particular the suburb of Fancheng, which lay on the opposite bank, was evacuated and the bridge between them demolished.

The siege began with an attempt by the Jin commander to persuade the Song to surrender Xiangyang, but all overtures were refused, in spite of the fact that there was great concern within the city over the amount of food that they had been able to stockpile. The selling of wine was banned, and the only alcohol that was permitted was given to the soldiers on the walls. All the other normal precautions were taken, notably against incendiary attack.

Catapults were the main artillery used from within the walls. A total of 114 machines were able to deliver stones or clay balls into the Jin lines. There were also 3,000 hand-held crossbows and a considerable use of 'thunderclap bombs', the soft-casing exploding devices hurled by catapult. As at Yubi, the attackers raised an earthen ramp, but as it had a wooden base the Song managed to burn it and cause it to collapse. An ambitious Jin scheme to divert the Han River also failed. The defenders frequently took the fight to the Jin in the form of night sorties, but the clearing and destruction of the inhabited areas round about had the unexpected result of creating a nuisance in the form of thousands of stray dogs, whose barking warned the Jin of any night attacks. So traps were set for the strays, which then ended up in the cooking pot. We also read of an attack from the Han River, probably by paddle-wheel ships:

> On the evening of the 25th day, taking advantage of the rain and overcast sky, the commander urgently sent Zhang Fu and Hao Yan to prepare boats large and small, more than 30 in number, enough to carry 1,000 crossbowmen, 500 trident spearmen, and 100 drummers, together with thunderclap bombs, and gunpowder arrows. They took cover by the river bank below the enemy's encampment … Then at the stroke of a drum the crossbowmen let fly a volley, and immediately following this all the drums sounded and the crossbows were fired. Simultaneously the thunderclap bombs and the fire arrows were sent into the enemy's camp.

It appears to have been the success of the scorched-earth policy that eventually persuaded the Jin to withdraw from Xiangyang, because there was simply a complete absence of wood for miles around for fuel or for making and repairing wooden siege machines. A similarly successful defence policy was adopted at De'an, including in this case the poisoning of wells. But as De'an's topographical location was different from Xiangyang the Jin besiegers were able to use mining, and succeeded in collapsing part of the outer wall. They may have done more, but were thwarted by ingenious listening devices in the form of a large earthenware pot, over the mouth of which was tightly stretched a thin hide. The pot was placed in a hole well below the surface of the ground and manned by troops with especially acute hearing. A set of such geophones, properly distributed, might locate with accuracy the sounds of subterranean activity at a considerable distance.

Incendiary warfare, so feared at Xiangyang, was used to good effect against the gates and inner buildings at De'an in the form of fire arrows and burning pots thrown from catapults. On one occasion the incendiary device literally backfired, because the Jin constructed a huge combustible tower filled with hay and straw which had to be dragged towards the gates by oxen. The Song defenders managed to set it alight before it was near enough to do any damage. Psychological warfare using arrow letters was also used, and on one occasion the attackers painted their face masks red so that they looked like devils. Flinging severed heads of prisoners into the city from catapults was a further way of trying to intimidate the garrison. Just as at Yubi, heavenly omens were sought and followed by both sides. Offerings were made to Guan Yu, the deified general from the Three Kingdoms Period who had become the Chinese god of war. He appears to have answered the defenders' prayers, because, just as at Xiangyang, the Jin finally withdrew.

Kaifeng, AD 1232

The city of Kaifeng, chosen as capital by the Song dynasty and then taken over by the Jin, saw much fighting throughout its history, the most celebrated occurring in the year AD 1232 when it was captured from the Jin by the Mongols under the famous general Subadai. We know quite a lot about the siege from a fascinating and graphic description of life in the besieged capital that was compiled by a Jin official. He wrote that Kaifeng had been in a state of shock as the Mongols approached, because their arrival was preceded by bad news of Jin defeats in the northern mountains where the soldiers were up to their knees in snow. After one such encounter a Jin commander had been discovered hiding in a hole in the ground and had been killed.

To raise the morale in Kaifeng the emperor deliberately made himself highly visible to his troops by touring the walls as the Mongol bombardment began:

> The last emperor personally left the palace and walked along the sections of the defence and was concerned about the troops. Therefore all the soldiers fought bravely, defying death. Whenever the emperor went out he was accompanied by only a few people and did not have his canopy carried above him so that the people could see him easily

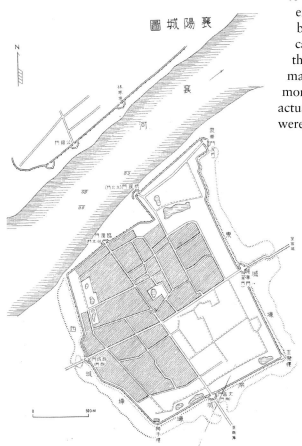

A plan of Xiangyang and its sister city Fancheng, the site of two fierce sieges by the Jin (AD 1206–07) and the Mongols (AD 1268–73). The two places now make up the modern city of Xiangfan. (After Ishihara Heizo)

圖城陽襄

At this stage in their development the Mongols do not appear to have possessed any exploding bombs, and their trebuchet missiles, flung from simple traction trebuchets operated by crews of hauliers, were confined to large stones 'like half millstones'. They were very effective, but the Jin could hit back with exploding bombs, and, 'The heavy pieces in the city – they were called "heaven shaking thunder" – replied. Wherever the northern army was hit fires started that burned many people to cinders.' Another account gives more detail about how the thunder-crash bombs were actually used. The fuses were lit, the trebuchets ropes were pulled and:

> There was a great explosion the noise whereof was like thunder, audible for more than a hundred li, and the vegetation was scorched and blasted by the heat over an area of more than half a mu. When hit, even iron armour was quite pierced through. Those who were not wounded by fragments were burned to death by the explosions.

Faced by these devastating weapons, the Mongols assault parties were forced to resort to desperate protective measures as they approached the city walls:

> Therefore the Mongol soldiers made cowhide shields to cover their approach trenches and men beneath the walls, and dug as it were niches each large enough to contain a man, hoping that in this way the

troops above would not be able to do anything about it. But someone suggested the technique of lowering the thunder-crash bombs on iron chains. When these reached the trenches where the Mongols were making their dugouts, the bombs were set off, with the result that the cowhide and the attacking soldiers were all blown to bits, not even a trace being left behind.

Another useful Jin weapon was the fire lance, which consisted of an ordinary spear to which was affixed a tube rather like a roman candle. It was lit by means of glowing tinder carried in a box at the soldier's belt and burned for about five minutes. When it was burned out its operator could use the spear for its conventional purpose.

In spite of the Jin's undoubted technical superiority in matters of explosives, the situation in Kaifeng rapidly deteriorated. An edict was therefore issued by the Jin emperor conscripting all males for the defence of the town walls on pain of death. Even the bookish students of Kaifeng, whom the government had decided were too weak for actual fighting, were eventually drafted into the trebuchet crews. This was too strenuous a prospect for some of them, and they petitioned the emperor to allow them to provide administrative support instead. Some got what they wanted, and the account continues:

> Furthermore, he ordered them to climb to the walls and let paper kites fly on which they had to fix a text asking the section of the population who had been forced to collaborate with the enemy outside to escape and return to the city in order to collect an official reward. Doing all these tasks the students could not avoid being exposed to the enemy's arrows and stone balls. Also, he made the students pull up the signal lanterns which signalled the start of sorties through the secret gates at night. If a lantern went out, the man responsible for it was executed. The students felt very bitter about this treatment.

A different account tells us that the string of the kites was cut so that they fell among the Mongol lines like a leaflet raid, but the Mongol besiegers scorned the whole process.

During the winter the Jin emperor, who had previously fled from Beijing, took the opportunity to flee from Kaifeng while he still had the chance. This caused such a catastrophic drop in morale that the officers left behind decided to surrender to avoid a worse sack than could be expected if the city was taken by storm. It was a wise decision, and after some slaughter the Mongols pursued the Jin emperor to nearby Caizhou where he had taken refuge. The Jin dynasty finally came to an end when he committed suicide in AD 1234.

Shaoxing, AD 1359

With the siege of Shaoxing by the rebels who were eventually to form the Ming dynasty, we move from the days of crossbows and catapults throwing exploding bombs to the employment of metal-barrelled cannon firing cannonballs. Shaoxing lies in Zhejiang province and was entirely surrounded by water because its own moat met several strategic waterways. For this reason the siege was conducted against a city that was never actually cut off from the outside world, and the rebels lacked the vast resources that would have been needed to overcome this. In their favour, however, was the fact that the rulers of Shaoxing were losing the confidence of their inhabitants. The city was only nominally loyal to the Mongol court in Beijing, and rebel influences were everywhere. Initially, at least, the resolve of the defenders held, encouraged by the atrocities

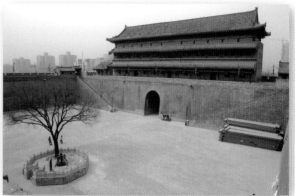

committed by certain irregulars that the rebels had with them. To further bolster the morale of the civilian population the Shaoxing commander actually encouraged the citizens to mount the walls and see for themselves how successfully the attackers were being driven back. This risky strategy was abandoned after a few weeks when it was found to have the opposite effect.

The most notable feature of the siege of Shaoxing was the innovatory use of cannon by both sides. The weapons were not large, and certainly could not smash walls down, but were effective against wooden structures such as gates and human targets. Gunpowder was manufactured inside Shaoxing itself, leading to a shortage of charcoal when all the trees within the city had been felled.

From this modern touch we may note a very ancient one, when a purple cloud was spotted over the besieged city. It was regarded as an auspicious omen that heralded a withdrawal of the Ming rebels. Prayers were offered to various deities, including ones to a deified emperor, but when the reply he gave was found to be discouraging his statue was pulled over in rage. Yet the omen was in fact to prove positive, because the rebels did indeed withdraw, although it was due to a pestilence that broke out in their camp rather than any divine intervention.

THE SITES TODAY

The Chinese were the world's greatest builders of walled cities, and it has been calculated that 4,478 walled cities were built, destroyed, abandoned or still used by the time of the Manchu conquest in AD 1644. Yet precious few remain. The past century has seen the destruction of hundreds of fine examples, usually in the name of progress, and often occasioned by the construction of railways and roads. Nowadays preservation and restorations are the keywords, so a journey is more than worthwhile, but a visitor has to be prepared to travel widely to see the best examples.

With every year that passes travel in China gets easier and its cities are more accessible, so any tourist advice in these pages will be out of date almost before it is printed. Organized tours are widely available, and nearly all take in Beijing. With the opening up of China as a tourist destination some now take in Pingyao in Shanxi. Tours of southern China usually include Suzhou, Hangzhou or Nanjing. The solo traveller is also well catered for, and I found travelling round China to be very easy, largely owing to the courtesy and helpfulness of the Chinese people. Domestic flights are readily available and can now be booked over the internet, while long distance buses will take the traveller to any of the sites mentioned here.

Beijing

In Beijing the Forbidden City provides the finest example in China of a palatial *cheng*. If possible go early, and enter by the back gate to the north. You will then have the sensation of walking round the eerily deserted courtyards before confronting the throngs in the main areas. The city walls of Beijing, once almost totally demolished, are now rising again. The south-eastern corner tower has been restored, as has a section of the walls adjacent to it along which a short walk may be taken. The tower itself houses a museum and an art gallery. The great Zhengyangmen gate houses an interesting and little-known museum about the walls of Beijing. The Museum of Beijing also has a splendid model of the city, while the fascinating National Military Museum has reproductions of siege weapons and numerous other items of interest, including paintings of attacks on walled cities.

Xi'an

Although the terracotta warriors are Xi'an's biggest tourist attraction, Xi'an's Ming walls are breathtaking, and are best seen by riding a bicycle round the

A small side entrance to the fortified village of Zhang Bi near Pingyao. The partial parapet above the wall may be seen in the top right-hand corner.

top of them. Bicycles are hired from offices helpfully located on top of the walls. The sheer scale of the long, straight sections is quite amazing. The vast inner courtyards of the *wengcheng* are most impressive, and there are reproduction siege machines dotted about. Several of the huge gate towers have been restored, and the two Wild Goose Pagodas are beautiful ancient structures. A fine model of Chang'an is on display in the otherwise rather strange Tang Paradise. This is a Tang Dynasty Theme Park for tourists, which includes some reconstructed buildings as well as sideshows, acrobatic displays and the like.

Kaifeng
The walls of Kaifeng are like Xi'an's on a smaller scale, and parts of them may be accessed. The reconstructed Song palace is quite interesting, with waxworks and historical objects. It is also a short taxi ride from Kaifeng to see the mighty Yellow River that has both defended the city and destroyed it on several occasions.

Pingyao
The finest Chinese walled city of all is the perfect Pingyao. Its entire Ming circuit is preserved with no high-rise buildings within it. Restoration has been carried out for several years, and considerable landscaping work was going on around the perimeter when I visited it in 2007. The admission fee for walking the walls is high, and the impression is given that this is an admission fee to the city itself, which it is not. It is still worth every penny, and provided one of the finest wall walks of my life, but as there are very few places where one may descend from the walls the visitor should check his watch before setting off on a very long trek. I chose
to complete the circuit over two days,

The view from the top of the access ramp of the southern gate of Nanjing looking towards the section of the city wall along the Qinhuai River.

one half being on top of the walls and the other walking outside. The buildings within the city are all of modest dimensions, and give the finest impression anywhere of old China. The visitor is strongly recommended to stay overnight within one of the small-scale private guest houses within the ancient walls.

Zhang Bi
Zhang Bi is accessible from Pingyao, and the only thing that spoils its perfection is the fact that the inhabitants have recently acquired the benefits of electricity. The chosen spot for the main distribution pole is right in the middle of the town. Nevertheless, this is a superb place to visit, including its very dusty tunnels. The temple and shrines are perfectly preserved, and the walls around the two entrances are as fine examples of Chinese military architecture as you will find anywhere. The fine details of its defences add greatly to one's knowledge of Chinese fortifications.

Zhengzhou
Only a short section remains of Zhengzhou's ancient walls, but one can actually climb onto this 3,000-year-old structure and walk along it past local citizens taking exercise.

Datong
Extensive earth walls and towers dating from the Northern Wei (c. AD 500) and Tang dynasties (AD 618–906) surround the city of Datong in Shanxi. The Northern Wei made it their capital in AD 398, by which time they had conquered the whole of northern China. Datong was also the capital of the Liao dynasty. The walls are almost square in shape, with two streets intersecting at a fine Ming dynasty drum tower. The old *hangtu* walls may be followed through an area of Dickensian squalor in this old coal mining centre. Again the walls may be climbed in places, and there is one interesting ruined corner tower. Unlike in well-restored Pingyao, you will probably be regarded as a considerable curiosity by the locals, who will be both bemused and delighted by your interest.

Nanjing
Nanjing has preserved several sections of its Ming walls. In the north-west some impressive sections can be seen at the so-called 'Stone City', where the city wall touches the Qinhuai River and the red sandstone bedrock provides the base for the soaring brick walls through which arches pass. The finest military site of all in Nanjing is, however, the southern gate, described in detail earlier. Approach it if possible from across the river, because this gives the complete experience of walking through its successive defensive courtyards. There is a small museum inside dealing with its construction history. From the top of the gate a short section of the wall may be followed along the river.

Suzhou
Suzhou has preserved much of its old character with canals and numerous famous gardens. The Panmen gate is worth a visit, and next to it is a small section of wall. The classic view of Suzhou is from the bridge leading to the Panmen, from where the relationship between the land gate and the water gate may be clearly appreciated. There is a tea room in the upper storey of the gate tower.

Penglai

Penglai, formerly Dengzhou, is an attractive place on the coast with a fine fortified harbour that is currently being restored. It is accessible from the city of Yantai, which has a convenient airport. There is much to see at Penglai, including several museums dealing mainly with the Chinese defeat of the *wako* and the heroic role of its native son Qi Jiguang. The fortifications are most impressive and may be thoroughly explored to their summit at the Penglai Pavilion, an ornate Qing dynasty structure. You may even be lucky enough to witness the 'Penglai miracle', a strange and rare atmospheric phenomenon when a mystical heavenly vision appears in the sky. It was once thought to be a revelation of the abode of immortals, but is now known to be a mirage of the city of Dalian on the Liaodong peninsula. This mundane explanation was finally confirmed in 1995 when the miracle included skyscrapers and cars.

Zhenhai

The coastal fortress of Zhenhai is accessible from Ningbo and is currently being restored. It is a stiff climb to the top, but a very rewarding visit. Curved Ming walls surround the top of the hill from where there is a good view across the estuary. The interesting Coastal Defence Museum, which deals largely with the activities of the *wako* and the 19th-century Opium Wars, lies next to the car park

BIBLIOGRAPHY

Balazs, Etienne (translated by Wright, H.M.) *Chinese Civilisation and Bureaucracy: Variations on a Theme* (Yale University Press, 1964)

Sen-Dou Chang 'Some Observations of the Morphology of Chinese Walled Cities', *Annals of the Association of American Geographers*, 60 (1970), pp. 63–91

Graff, David A. 'Meritorious Cannibal: Zhang Xun's Defence of Sui-yang and the Exaltation of Loyalty in an Age of Rebellion', *Asia Major,* 3rd series, 8 (1995), pp. 1–16

—— *Medieval Chinese Warfare 300–900* (London, 2002)

Haeger, John W. 'Li Kang and the Loss of K'ai-feng: The Concept and Practice of Political Dissent in Mid-Sung', *Journal of Asian History,* 12 (1978), pp.58–67

Higham, Robert and Graff, David A. *A Military History of China* (Oxford, 2002)

Ping-ti Ho 'Lo-yang A.D. 495–534: A Study of Physical and Socio-Economic Planning of a Metropolitan Area', *Harvard Journal of Asiatic Studies,* 26 (1966), pp. 52–101

Kierman, Frank A. *Four Late Warring States Biographies* (Wiesbaden, 1962)

—— and Fairbank, John K. *Chinese Ways in Warfare* (Harvard University Press, 1974)

Knapp, Ronald G. *China's Walled Cities* (Oxford, 2000)

Lorge, Peter *War, Politics and Society in Early Modern China 900–1795* (New York, 2005)

Needham, Joseph *Science and Civilisation in China*, Volume 4, Part 2: *Mechanical Engineering* (Cambridge, 1965)

—— *Science and Civilisation in China*, Volume 4, Part 3: *Civil Engineering* (Cambridge, 1971)

—— *Science and Civilisation in China*, Volume 5, Part 6: *Military Technology: Missiles and Sieges* (Cambridge, 1994)

—— *Science and Civilisation in China,* Volume 5, Part 7: *Military Technology: The Gunpowder Epic* (Cambridge, 1986)

Serruys, Henry 'Towers in the Northern Frontier Defenses of the Ming', *Ming Studies,* 14 (1982), pp. 8–76

Steinhardt, Nancy Shatzman 'Why Were Chang'an and Beijing so Different?', *The Journal of the Society of Architectural Historians,* 45 (1986), pp. 339–57

Trewartha, Glenn T. 'Chinese Cities: Origins and Functions', *Annals of the Association of American Geographers,* 42 (1952), pp. 69–93

Turnbull, Stephen *Siege Weapons of the Far East (1) AD 612–1300* (Oxford, 2001)

—— *Siege Weapons of the Far East (2) AD 960–1644* (Oxford, 2002)

—— *The Great Wall of China 221 BC–AD 1644* (Oxford, 2007)

Wallacker, Benjamin E. 'Studies in Chinese Siegecraft: The Siege of Yu-pi A.D. 546', *Journal of Asian Studies,* 28 (1969), pp. 789–802

—— 'Studies in Medieval Chinese Siegecraft: The Siege of Chien-k'ang, A.D. 548–549', *Journal of Asian History,* 5 (1971), pp. 35–54

—— (*et al,* eds.) *Chinese Walled Cities: A Collection of Maps from Shina Jokaku no Gaiyo* (Hong Kong, 1979)

—— 'Studies in Medieval Chinese Siegecraft: The Siege of Fengtian, A.D. 783', *Journal of Asian History,* 33 (1999), pp. 185–193

Wheatley, Paul *The Pivot of the Four Quarters: a Preliminary Enquiry into the Origins and Character of the Ancient Chinese City* (Edinburgh, 1971)

Cunrui Xiong, Victor 'Sui Yangdi and the Building of Sui-Tang Luoyang', *Journal of Asian Studies,* 52 (1993), pp. 66–89

Qiao Yun *Ancient Chinese Architecture,* Volume 10: *Defense Structures* (Vienna, 2001)

GLOSSARY

cheng	City wall, synonymous with city.
chi	Moat.
fang	Ward of a city.
feng shui	A system of divination.
guo	An outer wall to a city.
hangtu	Rammed earth.
li	A unit of length equivalent to 0.5km.
mamian	'Horse face', a tower that projects from a city wall.
mu	A unit of area equivalent to .067 hectares.
nuqian	Parapets around the top of a wall.
pi li pao	Paper-cased exploding bombs.
wako	Japanese pirates.
wengcheng	Complex gate systems.
wu bi	Fortified manor of the Han dynasty.
zhen tian lei	Exploding iron bombshells.

INDEX

Figures in **bold** refer to illustrations.

RELATED TITLES

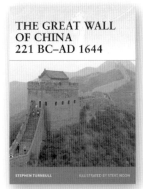

THE GREAT WALL OF CHINA 221 BC–AD 1644

FOR 057 • 978 1 84603 004 8

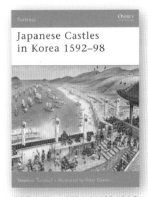

Japanese Castles in Korea 1592–98

FOR 067 • 978 1 84603 104 5

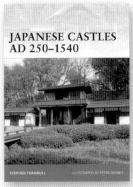

JAPANESE CASTLES AD 250–1540

FOR 074 • 978 1 84603 253 0

Genghis Khan & the Mongol Conquests 1190–1400

ESS 057 • 978 1 84176 523 5

Mongol Warrior 1200–1350

WAR 084 • 978 1 84176 583 9

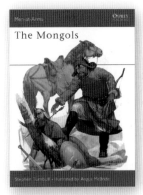

The Mongols

MAA 105 • 978 0 85045 372 0

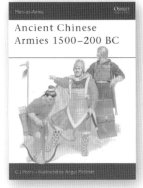

Ancient Chinese Armies 1500–200 BC

MAA 218 • 978 0 85045 942 5

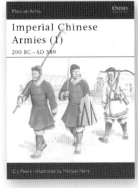

Imperial Chinese Armies (1) 200 BC–AD 589

MAA 284 • 978 1 85532 514 2

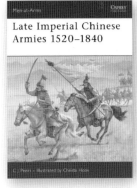

Late Imperial Chinese Armies 1520–1840

MAA 307 • 978 1 85532 655 2

VISIT THE OSPREY WEBSITE

Information about forthcoming books • Author information • Read extracts and see sample pages
• Sign up for our free newsletters • Competitions and prizes • Osprey blog

www.ospreypublishing.com

To order any of these titles, or for more information on Osprey Publishing, contact:

North America: uscustomerservice@ospreypublishing.com
UK & Rest of World: customerservice@ospreypublishing.com

Design, technology and history of key fortresses, strategic positions and defensive systems

CHINESE WALLED CITIES 221 BC–AD 1644

It has been said that in China a city without a wall would be as inconceivable as a house without a roof, and indeed, the Chinese built barriers to protect every kind of settlement, from the smallest village to the nation's Great Wall. Yet the finest examples of walled communities were China's walled cities, whose defensive architecture surpassed anything along the Great Wall. This book traces the evolution of the walled city, from the 3,000-year-old remains of beaten earth walls to the huge stone fortifications of the Ming dynasty. Illustrated with colour artwork reconstructions, maps and archive photographs, this book reveals the defensive structures of all the major ancient Chinese cities, and discusses how they protected entire communities, and not just castle dwellers, from attack.

Full colour artwork ■ Photographs ■ Unrivalled detail ■ Colour maps

US $18.95   UK £11.99
CAN $22.00

ISBN 978-1-84603-381-0

OSPREY
PUBLISHING

51895

9 781846 033810

GREEK FORTIFICATIONS OF ASIA MINOR 500–130 BC

From the Persian Wars to the Roman Conquest

KONSTANTIN S NOSSOV   ILLUSTRATED BY BRIAN DELF

ABOUT THE AUTHOR AND ILLUSTRATOR

KONSTANTIN S NOSSOV is a researcher in and advisor on ancient and medieval arms, armour and warfare, as well as the author of numerous books and articles on the subject. His particular areas of interest include the history of weapons, fortification and siege warfare. He has lived all his life in Moscow, Russia, and has travelled extensively in Europe, North Africa, South Asia, Asia Minor and the Far East. Konstantin has written several Osprey books, as well as other English-language titles and numerous books in Russian.

BRIAN DELF began his career working in a London art studio producing artwork for advertising and commercial publications. Since 1972, he has worked as a freelance illustrator on a variety of subjects including natural history, architecture and technical cutaways. His illustrations have been published in over thirty countries. Brian lives and works in Oxfordshire, UK.